Advance
Leadership in

MW01204753

Amy Gould

William L. Enyart,
*Major General, US Army (retired)
and former US Congressman*

LEADERSHIP
In Challenging Times

by
William L. Enyart
Major General,
US Army (retired)
and former US
Congressman

Leadership in Challenging Times
William L. Enyart
ISBN 979-8-9873861-9-4

© 2023 William L. Enyart

Cover art: © Can Stock Photo / merydolla
Cover design: Victoria Brzustowicz/Victoria B Creative

billenyart.com

This book is dedicated to the soldiers and airmen with whom I served. Brothers and sisters all. And to our families, who bore a far greater sacrifice than did we few.

ALWAYS READY!

Contents

Prologue

You say you want to be a leader? You need to buy this book. Why? Because it tells the lessons on life and leadership that I want my teenage grandson to know.

Although it's based mostly on my experiences commanding the thirteen thousand soldiers and airmen of the Illinois Army and Air National Guard, it applies to civilian leadership as well.

Buy this book if you have an MBA from Harvard business school. It will give you the perspective of the people who actually do the sweaty labor (whether at a desk or on the factory floor) in your organization. Buy this book if you just flunked out of the local state university and are struggling in a job you hate...welcome to the club. Been there, done that.

It is a book distilled from the lessons learned during my long and tortuous path from working class child of factory worker to wearing two-stars, commanding the citizen soldiers and airmen of the Illinois National Guard through its largest combat deployment since World War II. Not to mention leading weekend warriors through blizzards, floods and tornadoes, all the while fending off the, at best, erratic civilian leadership of former Illinois Governor Rod Blagojevich. Blagojevich is the Democratic half of the Illinois pair of governors imprisoned at the same time for misdeeds while in office.

Governors serve as their state National Guard's commander-in-chief, much like the President is the nation's military commander-in-chief. The Adjutant General (pronounced add-jew-tunt) is the military head of a state's National Guard, both Army and Air, much like the Chairman of the Joint Chief is the senior national military officer. The Adjutant General generally holds the federal rank of Major General, two stars. Enough about the bureaucracy, let's get to the story.

This book is not for the faint-hearted. It is a book for those who have failed. It is a book for those who are, on occasion, lost. It is a book for those who have thus far glided to success. Congratulations, you're about to step in a pile of you know what.

It is a book for those who truly care about where our lives, our businesses and our nation are headed, and, by the way, want to influence the course. It is a book for those who want to do the right thing, while not totally sabotaging their careers. It is a book of "lessons learned". That's an Army phrase.

The Army is big on "after action reviews" so "lessons learned" can be preserved to avoid making the same mistake twice. Think Pearl Harbor. Remember Pearl Harbor! Oh, but then we had 9-11 didn't we. Remember your mistakes! The more things change, the more they stay the same. Pearl Harbor, like 9-11, like the near financial collapse of 2008 were all clearly foreseeable, clearly avoidable and clearly a leadership failure. Pay attention!

This book is divided into three major sections, advice to junior leaders, advice to mid-level leaders and advice to senior leaders. The final chapter addresses post career advice. Most of the lessons apply to every level of leadership. If you don't think a lesson applies to you, read it again. Read it again a week from now, a month from now, a year from now, a decade from now.

If you re-read it a decade from now and it still doesn't apply, ask for your money back. Just remember to keep your receipt.

Chapter 1:
What I'm gonna tell you about leadership

"We don't believe in the American dream anymore. We don't believe you can be born poor and rise to success. The deck is too stacked against us."

Former director of national operations for the Democratic Congressional Campaign Committee, Jason Bresler, a then thirty-year-old millennial, said to my wife, Illinois Circuit Court Judge Annette Eckert. "Today, people can't do what the General has done."

What did he mean by "what the General has done"?

The DCCC sent Jason to Southern Illinois to run a very unlikely Congressional campaign. The Democratic candidate resigned, due to health reasons, five months before the election. Local Democratic office holders and leaders asked the state's National Guard commanding general to retire and run. That would be me.

The task looked more like the Alamo than D-day. The General had no campaign staff, had raised no money, and had never served in elected political office, with 150 days to go before the election. His opponent? The son of a billionaire, with state-wide name recognition from a previous run for lieutenant governor, and a well-organized, well-funded operation directed by national political figures.

The General? Grandson of sharecroppers, none of whom had more than an eighth-grade education; son of itinerant factory worker and dollar-store clerk who, as the rural Illinois saying goes, "didn't have a pot to piss in or a window to throw it out of" — and with his only seeming advantage over the young Republican, the General's decades of military experience.

With a pickup team of previously unemployed Democratic wannabe staffers who'd never worked on a winning campaign, dedicated volunteers, supportive family members, and a never-say-die attitude, the team essentially built an airplane while flying it at 35,000 feet to win the election.

1

This isn't a book about how to win an election. That's the only election I've ever won. It's a book about leadership. I'm just establishing my bona fides to talk about leadership.

Much of what I've learned about leadership I learned in the nearly thirty-six years I spent serving in the U.S. military. Some I learned practicing law in the courtrooms of Southern Illinois, not far from where Lincoln practiced. The rest I learned playing sandlot ball on empty lots in working class neighborhoods as a kid.

There is no magic formula disclosed in these pages. There are countless books on leadership. The American military dedicates years of training time in an attempt to instill it. You can even get a PhD from lots of universities in it. I hold an EBD degree in it. That is Earned By Doing.

So, this is a book containing the distillation of decades of experience serving with the greatest soldiers and airmen the world has ever seen, the finest military training the American taxpayer can provide, and just a little bit of independent reading.

Although this book is aimed at young National Guard officers and NCO's (non-commissioned officers), the lessons carry over to civilian life as well. Afterall, most National Guard members are part-timers with civilian careers.

The Army teaches young instructors to "tell 'em what you're gonna tell them, tell them, then conclude with what you told them."

Here's what I'm gonna tell you: The first section is advice, or maxims, about leadership for young leaders. The middle section is advice for mid-level leaders. The third section is advice for senior leaders. If you're a junior leader, or a wannabe junior leader, not even in the lowest rank of leadership yet, don't stop with the first section; read the whole damn thing. You may learn something.

On the other hand, if you're in the C-suite, don't skip to the final section. Read the whole damn thing. There are important lessons you should have and probably did learn as a junior leader that you better not forget once you're on the top of the pyramid.

There's a conclusion, too. I cribbed it from an old friend and mentor, Senator Alan Dixon, who, I'm sure, cribbed it from someone else. No sense reinventing the wheel, is there? You can skip to the end and read the conclusion if you want to, but then go back and read the damn book!

If you think I've forgotten something, if you think I've made a mistake, or if you just want to say "hello" send me an email: bill@ billenyart.com.

Chapter 2:
Show up to play the game

As you read this book, you'll discover the rules that I've used to climb the ranks from basic training enlistee to Major General and from Big Ten school flunkout to United States congressman with graduate degrees and an honorary doctorate. None of those maxims, rules, suggestions, or examples matter one damn bit if you don't master the single underlying requirement."

Show up.

That's right: Show up. You've got to show up to play the game. Maybe you don't like the rules. Maybe you don't like the refs. Maybe you don't like the shape of the ball. But the first thing you have to realize is that you, like it or not, are part of a tribe. Every tribe has its games. Every tribe has its hierarchies. Every tribe has its rules. Unless you want to be a hermit, you've gotta show up. You can't lead if you're not in the game. (And hermits don't have anyone to lead.)

I hear the whines now. "I don't like to play games. I wanna change the rules. The deck is stacked against me."

Life is a game because we humans make it a game. Life has rules because we live in tribal societies and to survive in any group larger than a family unit (maybe even there), we establish norms, and those norms become rules, written and unwritten. If you don't like the rules, change them, but you can't change them *if you don't show up.*

Sometimes things happen that cause you to leave the game. To change the card table you're sitting at. Let's take a look at Ulysses S. Grant. Grant, after graduating from West Point, served in the Mexican-American War as a junior officer. He was later forced to resign, while still a junior officer, for allegedly drinking on duty. He went on to fail at farming and other business ventures.

By the time the Civil War broke out, Grant was clerking in his father's leather goods store in Galena, Illinois. He was pretty clearly out of the game. Cashiered from the Army, middle-aged, broke, and undistinguished. He could easily have been embittered and said the hell with it, "I'm outta the game and I ain't gettin' back in." He didn't. He took a commission in the Illinois militia. And with an Army desperate for trained officers, even though he'd been out of the game for decades, Grant quickly rose to general and eventually commanded the Union Army to win the Civil War and go on to serve as president and write one of the best-selling books to that time, his memoirs. All of that because he showed up.

Had Grant not shown up, someone else would eventually have become Lincoln's Grant to provide the leadership needed to take the Union Army to success. But he did. In four years, a middle-aged, failed store clerk rose to command the Union Army to victory in the war that saw more American casualties than any war before or since. He gained the confidence and respect of our greatest American president.

Be Lincoln's Grant. Show up to play.

Chapter 3:
Set the course

I remember well the day my best friend from undergraduate school asked me what his career path should be. We were both about thirty. Both veterans, so we were a little older than our classmates as undergrads. At the time, I had just finished my law degree and he, his MBA.

He was angry with me when the best I could come up with was: "Chuck, cream will rise to the top, so you're gonna do well." This wasn't the answer he was looking for. He wanted me to set his goal for him so he could set a course.

Sorry, Chuck; only you can set your goal and then set your course.

It's probably a truism, but a truism for a reason. You must have a goal before you can set a course. For middle- and upper-class kids, it's in many ways easier to set a goal. Parents, grandparents, your social class set expectations, which you absorb and which become your goals. You're taught from an early age to have goals. College, career, 401k.

For working class kids, children of the working poor, it's a lot tougher. They generally don't have high expectations set for them. In fact, they often don't even have a concept of setting a goal.

Then there are the adults who put obstacles in the way of goal-setting. Particularly adults who deal with working class kids. There was my high school guidance counselor, who, when I told him, after receiving my ACT scores, that I wanted to go to Harvard, looked at me and said, "It costs $5,000 a year to go to Harvard." (This was in 1965.) My dad worked in the Caterpillar factory in Aurora, Illinois. Five thousand dollars was a year's UAW union worker's wages then.

I realize now that the guidance counselor, who was also the tiny high school's wrestling coach, sabotaged my goal. I'd been kicked off the football team for smoking, which didn't sit well with him, nor did the fact that I was a smartass. Enough reasons to pop a balloon.

A year later. A different guidance counselor. A young — barely older than me — attractive female encouraged me to think about the University of Denver. Why? I dunno. I guess she thought it sounded cool, since she attended teacher's college at Illinois State University on the flat lands of Central Illinois. I got the UD catalog. The price just to apply? Fifty bucks. Half a week's salary for my dad. Three to four weeks' salary from my part-time grocery bagger job. My limited goal-seeking mind couldn't comprehend spending that much money just to ask to get in.

What was my goal then? Complete college. Why? I believed that was the key to success.

I kept that goal for seven years. I eventually graduated from college after flunking out of the University of Illinois due to interfering, intermediate goals of beer, cards, and girls. Graduation came after joining the Air Force, rather than get drafted. That goal was a reach for a kid whose parents had never gone past high school and only one of whose grandparents had even finished the eighth grade.

What's the next goal? I didn't have one. I floundered. Got divorced. Got fired as a newspaper reporter. Luckily by the time I got fired, I had a new goal. Law school.

One of my mentors at the newspaper I'd worked for had a nephew who worked as a zoning lawyer in suburban Chicago. "Making a fortune," my mentor told me. Good enough for me. I was really tired of the near-poverty wages of a suburban newspaper reporter. New goal: Become a rich lawyer.

How'd I set that goal? I'd met a few lawyers as a newspaper reporter. I'd attended a few zoning board meetings. What the hell. The lawyers wore Brooks Brothers' suits, while I wore a cheap polyester sport coat from K-mart. They could afford to drink mixed drinks at the white-linen-table-cloth restaurant, while I swilled draft beer at the working man's bar. Time to move on up.

What's my point? Set a goal. Once you have a goal, it's possible to chart a course. If you don't have a goal, you can't begin to chart a course. The goal doesn't have to be a huge reach, but it does need to be a reach.

You must also be ready to re-chart your course to reach your goal. You will run into obstacles. Some self-made, some imposed by circumstance. You cannot let obstacles stop you. Flunking out of one of the best public universities in the country, when I had a full tuition scholarship to attend it, was sure as hell a self-made obstacle to my goal. But I never lost sight of my vision that a college degree would be my union card to a brighter future. Little did I know that that would not just be the first step, but a rather a hurdle that I had to get over to get to the next step to success.

Remember, too, that the goal you have at 16 won't be, or shouldn't be, the goal you have at 18, or 21, or 30, or 50. We'll talk about this more in Chapter Four, but you must reset the goal posts from time to time.

Having lived, more than one time, through the floundering that takes place when I didn't have a new goal, let me suggest that you move the goal posts back *before* you reach your goal. That simple process will save you a lot of time and mental energy.

When setting the goal, make it a clearly defined goal. It's much harder to chart a course to "I want to be rich" or "I want to win a Nobel Prize" than it is to set an initial goal such as "I'll save ten percent of my salary until I have $xxxx in the bank" or "I will get my BS in physics with honor-roll grades."

Sometimes those goals have to be a leap. As an enlisted airman in the Air Force, my goal wasn't the next promotion. I simply wanted to get out, get a degree, and make money. The poverty-level wages of a junior enlisted person were a huge driver there! But once I was commissioned a first lieutenant in the Army National Guard, my goal was two levels up. As a first lieutenant, I had my eye on major and what I needed to do to get there. As a major, the goal was colonel, not merely lieutenant colonel. You gotta keep that stretch going.

Chapter 4:
Begin the journey

Now that you've determined a goal and charted a course or at least you're thinking about a goal, so you can chart a course, let's begin the journey. And that's what life, like leadership is: a journey. Like all journeys, it is subject to detours, delays and, occasionally, disenchantment.

Let none of that discourage you, my friend. As the Alaskan said, "If you ain't the lead dog, the view never changes." So, let's set about changing your view.

There are three maxims in this chapter. Commit them to memory. If you learn nothing else from this book, learn them.

Maxim One: Persistence is the Parent of Success.

Maxim Two: Be a Boy Scout, that is, adopt the Boy Scout motto: Be Prepared.

Maxim Three: Failure is a learning process, not a prison sentence.

Maxim One: Persistence is the Parent of Success

Let's start with Lincoln and Grant. Two of my favorite leaders. They're two of my favorite leaders, because, like me, they served in the Illinois militia, what later became the Illinois National Guard.

Lincoln, as a young man, enlisted in the Black Hawk War and, after brief enlisted service was selected by his fellow soldiers to serve as a Captain. Lincoln has said of that selection, that of all his accomplishments, he was most proud of that acknowledgment by his fellow soldiers of his leadership skills.

Lincoln, like Grant, refused to let failure define his life. We know from history that both Lincoln and Grant failed multiple times in business. Lincoln lost elections to the state legislature, to Congress and to the Senate before eventually becoming President.

Grant, although a West Point graduate, was forced to resign his commission for allegedly drinking on duty. He went on to fail at farming and other businesses. At the time the Civil War broke out he was a middle-aged clerk in his father's leather goods store. But he went on from these failures to command the Union Army, which won the Civil War, and eventually be elected President.

What is the common denominator shared by these two presidents? Their refusal to let failures rule their lives. Major General John Fremont, early in the Civil War, said of Grant, he is a general of "dogged persistence" and "iron will".

There is an oft-seen poster detailing Lincoln's major failures in life which ends with "The difference between history's brightest accomplishments, and its most staggering failures is often, simply, the diligent will to persevere". So, maxim number one is: don't let failure stop you. No one can beat you if you keep getting up off the mat.

Let's think of it this way, when you're on vacation and get a flat tire, do you abandon the journey? Of course not, you change the tire, get your hands dirty doing so, and get back on the road.

After flunking out of the University of Illinois at the conclusion of my freshman year and enlisting in the Air Force, did I give up on my goal of a college degree? Nope. Shortly after my assignment to the 375th Aeromedical Evacuation Wing at Scott Air Force Base, Illinois, I began classes at the local junior college. Over the course of my two-year assignment there I earned a semester's worth of credits. I continued college part-time while overseas with the 824th Combat Support Group, so by the time I returned to the states and an honorable discharge I was able to complete undergraduate school in a year and a half. Persistence.

Not that there weren't a few bumps along the way, which leads us to a necessary corollary for persistence: Sometimes you need to find another way.

If you run into a brick wall, stop using your thick skull for a battering ram and go around, under or over the brick wall. Stop beating your head against the brick wall, step back and figure out another way.

Let's look at another historical figure who figured out another way. Winston Churchill became Prime Minister of Great Britain, on May 10, 1940. British, French and allied forces had collapsed before the German Wehrmacht. The British Army was surrounded at Dunkirk. Sixteen days after Churchill took leadership, a ragtag assembly of the British Navy, fishing boats and pleasure craft evacuated the British Army and some allied forces, while abandoning their equipment, from the European continent. Britain stood alone against a military that swept across Europe from Poland to the Atlantic in a matter of eight months.

Churchill refused to fail. To defeat the Nazi war machine, he had to not only persist, he had to find another way to defeat the enemy. He knew that Britain alone could not win. He had to persist against overwhelming odds and find a way.

He and the British hung on for a year and a half, until the twin Axis errors of attacking the Soviet Union and the United States brought the US and USSR into the war on Britain's side. Persistence, the parent of success.

Let me give you yet another example of persistence and finding another way. This time not of great world leaders, but rather ordinary folks, people like you and me. People who walk down the streets of an ordinary town like Belleville, Illinois, one of the industrial Illinois suburbs of St. Louis.

There were two young men who wanted to attend West Point. Each of the young men were athletically skilled, although not stars. Each were academically qualified, if not rocket scientist material.

Most appointments to West Point come via nomination by the local Congressman or Senator. Congressmen and Senators typically name a selection committee who review applicants' test scores, grades and extracurricular activities, then provide a rank ordered list of qualified candidates to the Congressman or Senator. There are some special categories, such as the children of Medal of Honor winners or star athletes, but most cadets enter through the Congressional nomination process.

Our first young man's grandfather was the county chair of the Congressman's political party. Although he didn't hold public office, he was one of the most powerful political figures in downstate Illinois and wealthy to boot. Because of his family's wealth, our first young man attended a prestigious, private St. Louis school where he received a prep school education that virtually guaranteed him admission to any Ivy League school. The Congressman nominated him and he was accepted to West Point.

Our second young man's grandfather was not particularly politically active, and, in fact, was suspected of favoring the other political party. Although certainly of the middle classes, the family was not wealthy. The young man attended a public high school, where he did well enough.

Realizing he was unlikely to get a Congressional nomination to West Point, our second young man, persistent as he was, needed to find another path. He had, after all, chosen his goal, with his initial course of a Congressional nomination blocked, he had to find a way around, over or under the brick wall.

Second young man researched the problem and found that there is a little-known path to West Point. There are fifty cadet slots reserved for National Guard soldiers who meet the qualifications. Because this program is little known and little publicized those fifty slots are seldom filled. Our second young man enlisted in the Illinois National Guard, completed basic training and, upon assignment to his infantry company, applied to West Point. He was accepted.

Postscript to the story. Our first young cadet grew bored with West Point, decided the military wasn't his goal after all, resigned from the academy after his second year and went to a West Coast university. Our second young man finished the academy, went to parachutist training and served in Afghanistan with the 101st Air Assault Division. After completing his tour of duty, he left the Army as a Captain and is now in law school. Where, by the way, his legal education is paid for thanks to the GI Bill and the State of Illinois veteran's tuition scholarship.

Over, under, around. Persistence. Find a way.

Maxim Two: Be a Boy Scout, Be Prepared

Be prepared. Be prepared for what? How do I know what to be prepared for? How do I prepare myself? All good questions. That's why you must have a goal. That's why you must chart your course. That's why you must be persistent.

That's also why you must be open to opportunity. When an opportunity arises, you must be prepared to seize it. And even more importantly you must be prepared to recognize it.

For the first twenty-five years after law school, I had a dual career. I spent Monday through Friday practicing law. During that two and a half decades, I built a modestly successful law practice. I loved going to work on Monday mornings because I loved helping people, putting the puzzle together of how to win their case and then getting paid to do it!

My other career was as a National Guardsman. One weekend a month and a few weeks a year I honed my skills as an infantryman, a military lawyer, as a staff officer and eventually as a general.

Honestly, I didn't much care for my active-duty time in the Air Force. As I would later say, it felt too much like "working for IBM". I was far too entrepreneurial to be locked into the timed promotions and pay increases of the active duty Air Force, especially due to the less than poverty level wages of a young enlistee in 1969. My pay dropped by eighty per cent when I enlisted, largely because the military didn't need to compete with civilian employment for new hires due to the draft. An E-1, or lowest ranking enlisted person, made just over $100 a month in 1969. Minimum wage then was $1.30 an hour, so an E-1 made about half the minimum wage, although we were provided food (albeit military food!) and a bunk bed in an open bay room with sixty other E-1s.

The great thing about the military, whether active duty or Guard, is that your preparedness path is laid out for you. It's easy to know what to do to get promoted. They tell you. Finish this military education course. Don't get into trouble. Wait the requisite number of months, or years, as the case may be and you'll get promoted. Of course, as you go up the ladder of success, just doing the minimum won't get you promoted, but nonetheless, the military, like most bureaucracies, sets the ladder for success in front of you.

If you're prepared and the person next to you, or just in front of you, or maybe just a little ahead of you isn't prepared, guess who gets that promotion. You do.

If you want that promotion, get thyself prepared. As a young major, I wanted to be promoted to lieutenant colonel. Major, by the way, is the most useless rank in the military, you generally don't command anything. You're usually a staff officer tasked with ensuring the success of the commander. Lieutenant colonel! Now that's a different story. You get to be in charge of things. Maybe a battalion commander, leading hundreds of troops. Much more gratifying.

Now to get promoted to lieutenant colonel in those days you needed to have completed at least one-half of the four-year command and general staff course and have served as a major for four or five years, not to mention have good OERs (OER is short for Officer Efficiency Report or a performance evaluation, received at least annually in the Army.)

So, one night a week for no pay, for four years, I attended a US Army Reserve school, forty-five minutes from home, in addition to my regular National Guard duties, not to mention practicing law, serving as assistant Scoutmaster and attending my kids' soccer games and school plays, to complete the course.

Bingo! The lieutenant colonel serving as the Staff Judge Advocate (or lawyer in command of the legal section) of the infantry brigade in Chicago retired. His deputy, whom we shall call George, assumed he would receive the job and the promotion. Alas for poor George, he wasn't prepared. Bill was. Bill got the promotion over the rather vociferous objection of George. Don't be George. Be Bill. Be prepared.

Now George did eventually get prepared and once Bill moved on George got the promotion. But George kept on not getting prepared and retired as a lieutenant colonel. Bill kept on getting prepared and retired as a major general. You know the drill, don't be George.

Maxim Three: Failure is a learning process, not a prison sentence

Failure is a learning process, but only if you use it to learn from your mistakes. You cannot and should not obsess about failing at a given task or goal, but rather analyze the failure. What mistakes were made? Was the approach wrong? Were there insufficient resources? Did you have a lack of allies? Did you have a sufficient grasp of the problem? Did you understand where the center of gravity of the problem is and did you direct the proper amount of resources to the center of gravity?

The new entrepreneurs of our internet age have the right attitude towards business failure. They approach business failure as a learning experience, rather than a mark of shame. Their mantra is set up a new business, if it fails, examine the failure for its root causes and move on to the next venture.

There is a mantra in the American military that "failure is not an option". Nonsense. Failure is a part of a learning process. Learn from failures and march on. Look at the American Revolution. The Continental Army lost battle after battle. Colonial victories against the British army were few and far in between, yet Washington persevered and ultimately prevailed.

A similar pattern can be seen in the American Civil War. Federal forces lost battle after battle. It wasn't until Gettysburg and Vicksburg, the twin battles of July, 1863, one in Pennsylvania and the other in Mississippi, that saw the Union armies prevail over the Confederate forces.

Although Gettysburg is far better known to the general public than Vicksburg, Vicksburg may be the more portentous battle for the young American republic. Grant's tenacity and success in commanding the Union forces at Vicksburg brought the cashiered officer, failed farmer, obscure Illinois clerk, returned soldier to the forefront of Lincoln's often desperate search for a general who could win.

Lincoln, himself, was well-acquainted with failure. He failed in business. He failed in politics, losing races for the state legislature, for United States Senate, for the Republican nomination for vice-president in 1856. Despite his lack of formal education, he was successful lawyer.

As with Lincoln or Grant failure is a learning process, not a prison sentence. Use it as a learning process, or if it's your subordinates who fail, use it to teach, not to flagellate, whether it's yourself or others. As I frequently told my young lieutenants, "You learn more from your mistakes than your successes."

Chapter 5:
Fall in love with your job—or get another one... really!

I've loved every job I've ever had, with the lone exception of active duty in the Air Force. I must confess I hated being in the Air Force. Why? It was the most boring job I've ever had. It was also the lowest paid and the least entrepreneurial.

Before all you Air Force vets start howling, let me explain. I enlisted as a nineteen-year-old, about to be drafted, college flunk-out. It was 1969 with the Viet Nam war at its height. All my working-class high school buddies were either enlisting or getting drafted.

Four of my closest friends from the Sandwich, Illinois, High School Indians football team joined the Air Force. After taking my draft board physical, I visited the military recruiters. I liked the Air Force guy the best and with four friends already in, I joined the Air Force, which, since I could type, promptly made me a supply clerk. With my lack of mechanical aptitude, it's a good thing they didn't make me a bomb loader or a jet engine mechanic, but being a supply clerk is not exactly a thrilling occupation.

Since the draft spurred hundreds of thousands of young men to join the military, they didn't have to pay much. My pay took an eighty per cent drop upon enlisting, which barely left me enough money to make the car payment on my used Ford, with just enough left over for a carton of cigarettes. With the agonizingly slow, lockstep time-in-grade requirements for promotion and with it, pay increases to a livable wage, made me a very unhappy camper.

But since leaving the Air Force and finishing undergraduate school and law school on the GI Bill (with a sincere thank you to American taxpayers), I've been a sportswriter, police beat newspaper reporter, lawyer, part-time college instructor, business owner and executive, part-time Army National Guard officer, full-time National Guard commander with 13,000 troops and a United States Congressman. Loved every one of them.

While raising my two sons, I frequently told them, "Find a job you love and you'll never work a day in your life." I loved going to work because I loved my jobs. I can't say that I ever really considered them jobs. Jobs were the things I did to get through school. Things like working on the welding line at Caterpillar or cutting old, rusty barges into scrap steel or cleaning toilets on the night shift in downtown St. Louis. Now those are jobs.

Getting paid to go to Cardinals baseball games and write about it, or firing a thirty-caliber machine gun out the side of a Huey at five hundred feet or putting the puzzle of facts and legal procedure together to win legal disputes, those were all fun and games, compared to a real job.

Not that there weren't some bad aspects to each of those professions. Sportswriters don't get paid much; lawyers have to deal with the occasional cranky judges, always stressed clients and the sometimes difficult opposing lawyers; Congressmen have to raise money for reelection campaigns and soldiers get to go to scenic places that aren't on the cruise ship itinerary, but I loved every one of them.

I drove my secretaries crazy every Monday morning because I was so happy to come to work. You see it wasn't work for me, it was fun. Find that career. It really is fun when you love what you do.

When it stops being fun, leave. Life is too short to hate what you're doing.

Chapter 6:
First leg of the journey

Congratulations, you've got your immediate goal, your stretch goal and you've set your course. Let's explore what maxims govern the first leg of your journey. And make no mistake, success, like life, is a journey, not a destination.

Maxim 1: Constantly raise the bar.

That doesn't mean you must raise the bar every day, but you must raise the bar each time you succeed. You must look two steps ahead. Most critically you must have the new goal in mind before you reach your current goal. If you don't, you'll flounder or simply spin the wheel trying to find a course you haven't set.

Ironically, it's most important to have an alternative goal should you fail. As a young lawyer, I fell into a choice political patronage position, right out of law school. Through a combination of dumb luck and being in the right place at the right time, with the right credentials, educationally and politically, I was selected as outside counsel for a new local government entity at a pay rate that made me the highest paid graduate in my law school class, even though I was one of the lowest ranked academically. Parenthetical note: Since graduation, no one has ever asked me where I ranked academically in my law school class, but then I've never sought to work in a corporate firm or as a law professor.

I was on top of the world, until four months later, when my political patron decided he wouldn't run for re-election. The political calculus immediately changed. With the change in political winds, it didn't take me long to realize that with a new administration I wouldn't be able to hang on to my lucrative position.

What to do? What to do? The Democratic candidate for state's attorney (county prosecuting attorney) in the small rural county I lived in dropped out of the race. I'm less than a year out of law school, but who cares! The Democrats needed a candidate. I knew I'd need a job. I grabbed the opportunity and started running.

Did I mention this was May and the election in November? Did I mention my Republican opponent was a third-generation farm boy there and I'd moved in six months earlier? Did I mention this was 1980, the year of the Reagan landslide and I was running as a Democrat? Nonetheless, I began knocking on every door in the county of twenty thousand souls.

Five months later, when the votes were tallied, I lost by 412 votes. A couple of weeks later I was fired from my political patronage legal position. Shit happens.

House payments, car payments, student loan payments and no plan B. It wasn't a pretty sight. I may not have been as depressed as Lincoln, but damn sure close. What I didn't realize at the time, is that that failure laid the foundation for later success. Some of the many voters I shook hands with became clients. One of those clients came to me with a personal injury suit that eventually paid off all my debts and set me on the path to financial freedom.

Failing in that election also led me to join the Army National Guard as a JAG officer (Judge Advocate General or Army lawyer), which gave me a whole new set of options for a path to success.

Had Lincoln not failed at business would he have become a successful lawyer? Had he not lost the Senatorial election in 1858 to Stephen A. Douglas would he have become President?

Had Grant not been cashiered from the Army for drinking would he have become an Illinois militiaman and slogged his way to victory in the Army of the West, bringing him to that failure Lincoln's attention?

The point is that success comes to those who, in spite of failure, reset their compass and continue the journey.

Maxim 2: Stay awake! You won't know when opportunity arises if you're not awake.

It's ok to take a twenty-minute nap once in a while, but you gotta be awake to see the occasional brass ring dangling in front of you. What's your nap? Video games? Netflix bingeing? Alcohol? Drugs? Job? Social media? Cell phone? All of those, and more, numb your mind. All of those keep you from being awake and putting the pieces of the puzzle together.

Leadership is about having a vision and implementing that vision. If your mind is numb, if you're asleep, it's a whole lot tougher to see the vision. It's a whole lot tougher to recalibrate the course.

17

Maxim 3: Mentors are like guideposts, so know the landscape a little before you pick a mentor. Corollary: know when you've gone past the guidepost so you know when it's time to pick a new one.

New job? There's always someone there who wants to be your friend. Someone who wants to show you around. Someone who wants to gossip about the boss, about co-workers, about how screwed up management is. Is that the person you want as a mentor?

Don't latch on to the first person you meet at the new job as your mentor. Take the time to survey the territory. You may want to take the country roads rather than the interstate, and that's okay, but you don't want a dead-end journey, so pick your mentor like you pick your guideposts, with care to ensure they point in the direction your compass tells you to go.

Maxim 4: Nobody likes a springbutt—not even the teacher, or, know when to wave your hand with the answer. Corollary: God gave you one mouth and two ears for a reason.

Springbutt: definition: military speak for that person we've all met, who has a comment or answer at every seminar. Springbutt comes from the appearance of a spring in their butt which propels them out of their seat to answer a question or render a comment.

If you have this tendency, and most who do, won't recognize it, sit on your hands until the instructor or seminar leader asks the question, or for a comment, at least twice, surveyed the room with growing desperation and needs a life line. If you pop your hand in the air, wiggle in your seat with anxiety to answer first every time, your peers will hate you. The leader will learn to ignore you and you'll get no extra points for saving the instructor from your classmates' ignorance.

The corollary to this advice is, as my grandmother said, "God gave you two ears and one mouth for a reason". Listen more, talk less. Unfortunately, the people who need this advice won't hear it because they're still talking.

When I commanded the Illinois National Guard, the senior chaplain, who regularly visited my office to report on the well-being of our troops, told me: "General, in the seminary they taught us that the perfect sermon is seven minutes long. Long enough the parishioners think they got their money's worth, but not so long as to bore them." Take that advice to heart. Give people their money's worth but don't, for God's sake, bore them. How can you get a message across to bored listeners?

This virus infects some CEOs, professors, generals, ministers and political leaders. They believe their words are so inspiring they must give all of them to the audience.

During my spectacularly short Congressional service, a very senior political leader flew out to Southern Illinois on a bitterly cold February day to speak at America's Central Port, Granite City, Illinois, in support of the Obama administration's program to redevelop American infrastructure. After a brief tour of the port, a thinly disguised campaign rally took place in a huge unheated tent outside a union hall.

Local Democratic office holders, activists, union members and the general public gathered an hour or more before the speeches. As the area's Congressman I introduced the prominent political leader. My speech, a mere prelim, took two or three minutes. Even though we on the stage had heaters blowing warm air on us, I was freezing. The packed audience, standing on the frozen ground, slapped their gloved hands in an effort to stay warm.

These people were supporters! They were Democrats! They were there to see and be seen with their hero! They wanted the chance to get a selfie with their internationally known, political leader.

Teleprompter to the right of him. Teleprompter to the left of him. No topcoat, no hat, no gloves, remember the heaters were blowing warm air on him, our unnamed leader began speaking. And speaking. And speaking. Forty-five minutes later, after extolling every policy point the hapless Washington DC speechwriter could possibly put in, our speaker wound down. My butt hurt from the steel folding chair. My mind was numb from talking point, succeeded by talking point, succeeded by policy pronouncement. The audience, loyal Democrats, loyal citizens, stayed to the bitter, bitterly cold, end.

The politician, God bless him, stayed for another forty-five minutes, shaking hands and posing for photos, which is what the audience really wanted, not forty-five minutes of policy blather.

The speech might well have been perfect in front of DC policy wonks, or university political scientists, or foreign trade representatives, all in a comfortable conference room with padded chairs and nearby rest rooms. It sure as hell didn't work for a twenty-degree February day in a tent to an audience of union steelworkers and Democratic activists.

Lesson learned: 1. Know your audience! 2. Never, never, NEVER bore your audience. 3. Seven minutes is enough! 4. If you're senior enough to have a speechwriter, you tell them what you want to talk about, don't let them tell you what to read!

It's a simple rule: Talk less, listen more.

Maxim 5: Learn from everyone. Corollary: Some people are smarter than they look, or as gramma used to say: "you can't tell a book from its cover."

Okay, we all know you're the smartest person in the room, otherwise you wouldn't be reading this book. Now that we've acknowledged that fact, do you know how to lay brick? I thought not. How you gonna learn to lay brick? You could watch YouTube. You could read a book. Not much feedback from those methods. Nope, the best way is to find a master mason to teach you. Someone to provide you the necessary feedback when you screw it up.

When you go into a new leadership position, whether it's a junior position or CEO, your subordinates will, in all likelihood, have a far better idea of how to lay bricks than you do. Take the time to learn a little bit about bricklaying before you change the entire process.

You say: "But I don't wanna be a bricklayer." I know you don't, but you have to understand that bricklayers are craftsmen. They like what they do. They take pride in what they do. They are good at what they do. Your vision may be to build a beautiful house, but you can't do it without bricklayers. Find that master mason in your organization. Use his or her knowledge of the process to help you build your vision.

Maxim 6: Don't be a "PowerPoint Ranger"

So, what's a PowerPoint Ranger? Another military speak. Every organization has them. PowerPoint Rangers are the folks who are terrific at the minutiae of explaining (or sometimes misstating) plans and goals. They spend hours developing elaborate presentations. They never accomplish anything in moving towards the goal. They never develop the plan. They never get their hands dirty doing the actual work.

Rangers are the folks who paint their faces with camo and crawl through the swamps to attack the objective. PowerPoint Rangers are the ones who spend their lives fooling around with slide presentations.

If you're a PowerPoint Ranger, you'll stay a PowerPoint Ranger. Trust me, the commander knows the difference. Paint your face. Crawl through the swamps. Attack the objective. Find somebody to be your PowerPoint Ranger, but don't you be a PowerPoint Ranger, unless that's what you want to be, in which case, put this book down and go play with your computer.

What we're also talking about with PowerPoint Rangers is the danger of overspecialization. In the military, officers through the rank of colonel are assigned to specialties. Those specialties are called MOS for military occupational specialty. Some folks are logisticians, some are medical, some are infantry or artillery, the list goes on. But once an officer is promoted to general, they no longer have a specialty. That's why they're called generals. They're generalists, not specialists. They're expected to have a general knowledge of how things work so they can set the goals.

You want to be a general, that's why you're reading this book, so be good at your specialty so you can become a general and move beyond your specialty.

Maxim 7: Who defines your success?

If you answer anything other than: "I do", you're wrong! Now, of course, there are those who will argue this is incorrect. They ask: what about parents? what about teachers? what about peers? What about bosses? Nope. Nope. Nope. Nope.

All those folks only define your success if you let them. They may have their standards for what your success is, but ultimately that nagging little voice in your head defines it. Now, you may have to meet certain standards of others to gain their approval. In order to get a raise. In order to get an A. But you define success for yourself.

Let's talk about how we define success. The Army starts teaching its officers at a junior stage that the seventy per cent solution on time is better than the one hundred per cent solution late. Why?

First: in the real world, there is never a one hundred per cent solution. There are variables you cannot control. There are unanticipated events. Your opponent always has a vote.

Second: If you delay taking action until you have the perfect solution, your opponent or events are in control.

As a leader, you will be criticized for only having a seventy per cent solution. Don't let that worry you. You will be criticized by someone, somewhere, for your action or your inaction either way. Remember President Lincoln. Generations of historians hail him as our greatest president, but during the Civil War he was despised by many, criticized by virtually all and made decisions resulting in death and destruction to save our nation. He had no one hundred per cent solution. He didn't even have a seventy per cent solution until he found Grant, whose dogged determination provided a seventy per cent solution to defeating Lee and ending the Civil War.

Maxim 8: (My very favorite saying) Don't ever kick a horse turd in this town, somebody's uncle is under it.

I learned this maxim from my greatest mentor. Colonel Jack Gianninni. Colonel Jack, as he was universally known among the lawyers of the hard-scrabble industrial Illinois east suburbs of St. Louis, served thirty years in the Air Force. A three-war fighter pilot, World War II, Korea and Viet Nam, Colonel Jack was a fierce opponent in the divorce courts, a raconteur of the first order and a colorful writer. He was known to take a television set in exchange for his fee when a client had no money, yet yearly gave tens of thousands of dollars to the financially strapped local schools to ensure that their working-class students had modern technology in their classrooms.

Colonel Jack's words of wisdom simply mean, don't criticize anyone. You never know what their ties in the community are. You will get transferred. You will move to a new community. You will take a new position, where you are learning the network of relationships that binds people. Don't damage your newly found network by criticizing those who've long been part of the landscape.

Maxim 9: When you walk your dog, always carry a plastic bag. In fact, always carry a plastic bag.

Two reasons: 1. The dog shit you pick up today is the turd you won't step in tomorrow (or your boss won't step in this afternoon) and 2. You never know who will see you pick up that litter. So, whether you're a buck private or a general, bend over and pick it up. If you're the buck private, you may impress the general, and if you're a general, you'll sure as hell impress the private.

Not to mention you will feel just a little bit better knowing you've made the world just a little bit better place for having done it. Those mornings when I work out at the local YMCA, I always carry a plastic grocery bag to stuff the McDonald's cups, beer cans and detritus found on city streets into. I take a different route walking the five blocks home so I get the opportunity to clean up our town just a little more. The self-righteousness you will feel will make your entire day feel better. 1. You worked out. 2. You picked up after those slobs who littered our town. 3. You put one (or more) of those nasty little plastic bags to good use, saving a sea turtle from eating it!

No one's praised me for it yet, but I sure do get to praise myself for it!

Maxim 10: Have your lifeboat ready.

When the ship goes down, no one is going to care about your lifeboat like you will. Most people will only care about their lifeboat. If you don't have yours ready, guess who's going to be floundering in the cold, deep water.

Know now that sooner or later the ship will go down. Whether it's a company buyout, a change in technology that makes your skill set that of a harness maker, a bankrupt company or just plain bad luck, it will happen.

How do you build a lifeboat? Always, always, always, have your FU money laid back. What's your FU money? That's the money you need when your boss tells you to do something that inspires the response "FU"!

Maybe it's a command that violates your moral code (more about that later), maybe it's a transfer to a place you really don't want to go, maybe it's a demotion or a promotion you really don't want to take. In any event, it's an event that inspires those famous last words.

How much money is enough to say FU? That's up to you to figure out, but how much do you need to survive until you can find a new job? How much to meet your minimum expenses? How long will it take you to find a new job or otherwise earn enough to meet your expenses?

That number may be a whole lot less than you think, if you keep your debt and your expenses low. Lower than your income! Lower than your peers. Lower than the constant push to consume that you receive daily. There are lots of books and articles out there on how to save money not buying Starbucks every morning. I won't rehash any of that here. Go buy one of those books, or better yet, get a library card and borrow as many as you like for free.

Maxim 11: You're selling your time, not your soul.

I mentioned above that one of the things that may sink the Titanic is a directive from above that you do something for work that violates your moral code. Maybe it's an order to screw customers, maybe it's cutting corners that you know shouldn't be cut, maybe it's to out and out lie about your product. Whatever that command is, remember you're making a living, not selling your soul.

Unless you are selling your soul, in which case you're reading the wrong book, you're selling your time, your effort, your energy, your skills. You can quantify what those are worth. Selling your soul, that's a different matter. That's tough to quantify. If a boss, or a company or a customer is demanding you sell it, it's time to check your lifeboat, say FU and jump.

One final thought on having your lifeboat ready. As a young lawyer, a far more experienced, wily old lawyer and I were trying a nasty custody case at Christmas time (divorce cases with kids are always nasty at Christmas). The trial went on for several days. Each side hopelessly angry. Each of the lawyers knew we'd never be paid the worth of our time and effort.

The wily, old lawyer desperately wanted to resolve the case. Year-end rapidly approaching he had other cases worth far more that he could be working on. Known as a profligate spender, he had the IRS and debt collectors baying at his heels. "Bill", he said, "always remember, a broke lawyer is a bad lawyer." Meaning a broke lawyer will settle a good case for far less than what it's worth because he needs the money now. That maxim applies no matter your profession.

Years later, I offered to give that same wily, old lawyer some office furniture I had in storage, while IRS agents carried his possessions out of his office. He couldn't follow his own advice. Don't be a bad lawyer (insert your profession here). Keep your lifeboat patched, full of air and ready to launch.

People who don't have lifeboats drown. Don't drown.

Chapter 7:
Five Things People Fear

As a leader, you must understand what people fear. Unspoken fears motivate people in two ways. The first is to resist; the second is to do things to avoid the fear.

I'm not talking about fear of heights, or fear of spiders, or fear of snakes, all of which are common phobias. Nor am I talking about fear of physical harm. I am talking about engrained psychological fears that most people don't know they have and most would argue that they don't have.

The five fears I find most important to overcome are: change, success, failure, the unknown, and excommunication/rejection. These fears are why people don't rise higher in leadership positions and why there are so few entrepreneurs and great change agents. Important note here: the popular perception is that there are lots of entrepreneurs. Statistics puts the lie to that belief. In 2019 according to Statista, there were 0.31 per cent new entrepreneurs per adults in the US, or 310 out of every 100,000 adults. According to the Atlantic magazine, world-wide the US ranks second to last in the number of new startup businesses. (An important corollary here: don't always believe the popular perception.)

Fear of change. Most people hate and fear change. We become accustomed to our ruts. We like our routines. We drive the same way to work every day. We go to the same places on vacations. We stop at the same coffee shop every morning. Why? Because it's easy. It's routine. It's a habit.

As a leader, you will receive resistance, spoken or unspoken, when you institute change. Know it, embrace it, and work around it. When you find that rare person who doesn't fear, resent, or hate change, make that person a key part of your team. They will help drive the changes that you see as necessary to success.

Fear of success. Many people also fear success. Why in the world are most people afraid of success? Perhaps it's fear of change. Perhaps it's fear of taking the risks necessary to succeed. Perhaps it's the flip side of the failure coin.

But the simple fact is that most people are afraid of success. Success elevates people above their peer groups. Success makes you a target for those less successful. Success means you're climbing the pyramid and as you rise on that pyramid, the penalty for falling increases. Success for the average person represents change, and change represents danger. Thus, the average person declines success. They avoid the discomfort of facing their unspoken, unknown fear.

Fear of failure. Fear of failure is why people fear success. It is why people fear risk. Failure is painful. We are taught from an early age by our bodies and by our parents to avoid pain. Thus, most people avoid taking risks to avoid the pain of failure.

Fear of the unknown is closely akin to fear of change. Change is often feared because it leads to the unknown. People being led into the unknown are on high alert, watching for the sabre-toothed tiger to attack. To get past this fear, your people must have confidence that you, the leader, know where you are leading them.

Fear of excommunication/rejection. People are, by and large, herd animals. We follow the herd. We are social creatures. We want the acceptance of our peer group. To work too stridently for change, to seek success too boldly, to fail too spectacularly runs the risk of excommunication from the peer group. It runs the risk of rejection. We all fear rejection. We all seek acceptance.

Know that you have these fears. Don't let them cripple you. Pick up that paper and swat the spider. Step out onto that ledge. Grab the snake behind its head. Yes — if you succeed, you will leave your peer group behind. You will develop a new peer group. As you rise higher on the pyramid, you will have the opportunity to see further. When you fail, and you will, learn from those lessons so you avoid repeating the mistakes that led to failure.

Learn to detect fear in those around you. As part of that learning process, learn to assess whether that fear represents a real danger or can be safely disregarded. Having been in a few places where people would gladly have killed me, I've developed a fear-o-meter to detect fear in others. I recommend you do so, too.

When your fear-o-meter detects fear, it is up to you to coach your subordinates through it. That's why it is critically important that your subordinates view you as "an honest broker". If they trust and respect you as a leader, they MAY follow you through their fears. If they don't respect and trust you, they sure as hell WON'T.

Chapter 8:
Damn, I got promoted. What do I do now?

Middle management: heaven or hell?

Congratulations: You've been promoted to the ranks of middle management. Your new position can resemble heaven or hell. Especially since so many factors are out of your control. As a middle manager, you have little control over who your supervisors are, and probably not a lot more control over who your subordinates are and virtually no control over corporate policies. The only sure thing you can control is your approach to the new job and your reaction to others and corporate policies.

Let's start at the beginning with your promotion.

Maxim 1: Relax

Everyone who gets promoted feels that "What do I do now?!" way. If they don't at first, they soon will. Unless it's truly an insignificant promotion (that is, they gave you a new title, but no new responsibilities, just to make you feel good), it takes eight to twelve months to learn the ropes.

If you've read this far, you know, or should know, the Peter Principle, the principle that says: Sooner or later, every leader hits their level of incompetency. It's not likely that you've hit your level of incompetency … yet.

Maxim 2: Don't Reinvent the Wheel, Reinvent Its Use!

Think Zuckerberg and Facebook. He (and friends) took a process that Harvard University used to introduce new students and moved it to the Internet age, changing the way billions of people interact and making billions of dollars in the process.

Don't hesitate to take a process you see and twist it just a bit, to make it work better, apply it to a different set of facts, use it in a way it hasn't been used in the past. It doesn't have to change the world, but using an old process in a new way can bring you to the attention of people who can change the trajectory of your career.

Let me give you a personal example. Many years ago, I was a young lieutenant on National Guard summer maneuvers in the mosquito-filled woods of Wisconsin. Each summer, the Guard flew a group of civilian business and community leaders up from Illinois to observe our training. The public relations gesture was designed to improve employer support of our part-time soldiers, who frequently miss work due to training, floods, blizzards, or overseas deployments.

The visitors stumble out of the dark, noisy metal interior of a Viet Nam era, four-engined, propeller-driven C-130 Hercules. Down its metal ramp, into the bright sunshine of a Wisconsin summer day. Bumbling and stumbling about as civilians, taken out of their normal operating environment, are wont to do.

The brigade commander, a full colonel (a big deal in military life, for you civilians), gives them a pep talk about the adventures they'll have this day, watching their soldiers train. Surrounding the group is a flotilla of jeeps and open-bed olive-drab trucks. Camouflage-clad drivers leaning against the vehicles.

How in the world do we get the correct civilians in the correct vehicles so as to get them to the various training sites on the fifty-thousand-acre fort that they're supposed to visit? Each of the civilians has received an agenda, detailing where they're going. The agenda has a number for the driver they're assigned to. Each driver has a 3x5 index card bearing that number.

Unfortunately, no one told the drivers what to do with their cards. Some have theirs tucked in a pocket (one of the many pockets on a camo uniform!), some have it tucked in a folder, some have it lying on the seat of the vehicle. One — only one — has it tucked into the headband of his helmet, easily visible for all to see.

As the colonel is speaking, I grasp the problem of civilians finding their drivers and vehicles. This will be a total screw-up.

How to solve it? The colonel ain't gonna be pleased if he sees a milling mass of civilians attempting to sort themselves out!

The headband-wearing NCO has the solution, but doesn't know it. He just stuck the card there to get it out of the way. The colonel ends his briefing. To his surprise, the young, dumb lieutenant (lieutenants are universally viewed by NCOs and senior officers as young and dumb) takes charge.

During the colonel's speech, the lieutenant hustled from driver to driver, telling each of them to put the number-bearing 3x5 card on the front of their helmet, held in place by the three-eighths–inch elastic helmet band that holds the camo cover in place.

"Can I have your attention, please?" the lieutenant proclaims to the uneasy civilians, who clearly don't know what to do next. The colonel does not appear pleased at the brash young lieutenant taking command of the situation. Lieutenants, who are four or five echelons below full colonels, don't usually do that immediately upon a colonel's concluding remarks.

Addressing the crowd, the lieutenant says, "You all have a number on your agenda. Your assigned driver is wearing that number on his helmet. Please walk over to that driver now. He will be your driver all day."

Civilians provided with clear instructions. No milling about. No wasted time. Surprised look on colonel's face due to the lieutenant's quick solution to the vexing problem of disorderly confusion.

No big deal, right? Au contraire, my friends. The colonel became a one-star general, then a two-star general. He didn't forget the lieutenant's quick solution to a problem. That quick solution set an image of the lieutenant as a problem-solver. A year or two later, when the colonel needed to fill a sensitive and upwardly mobile position, he remembered the young lieutenant and tapped him for the job. Sometimes little things bring order out of chaos. It just takes the right person seeing the necessary tweak to a process to make that happen.

Be that person who is a problem-solver, not a problem-maker, nor a problem ignorer.

Moral question: Should the lieutenant have given credit to the NCO who unknowingly gave the lieutenant the solution? If so, when and to whom?

Damned if I know. Go ask the chaplain. That NCO probably doesn't know it, but by wearing that 3x5 card in his helmet band that sunny summer Wisconsin day, he set me — that lieutenant — on the path to becoming a two-star general. I gave him a nod in thanks that day. He dipped his head in acknowledgment.

Maxim 3: Learn to Recognize Opportunity

As a junior leader, you must develop your senses to recognize opportunity. In the previous maxim, you read about the young lieutenant who spotted a problem about to develop, saw a solution, took charge, and implemented the solution.

It was a small problem and an easy solution. It required only three steps: 1. Spot the problem as it is developing, but before it happens; 2. See the solution; 3. Take the initiative to implement the solution quickly. A fourth step, which you likely will have no control over, is to have a senior leader witness your three steps.

How do you learn to recognize opportunity? Pay attention. Pay attention to processes. Is the process operating smoothly? Is the process going to provide you with the intended result? Is the intended result the result that is needed?

A flaw at any one of those stages is an opportunity for you. An opportunity to be a hero. A hero is simply someone in the right place, at the right time, who takes an action that others wouldn't, usually because others aren't aware of the necessary action.

Don't be concerned about being a hero, because you won't even know you're going to come out like one; you're just trying to solve a problem. Solve the problem and you'll be a hero to someone.

Nine times out of ten, the people whose problem you solve won't even be aware of what you did to help them. The civilians weren't aware of the oncoming problem the young lieutenant saved them from, but the colonel sure as hell was. Right place, right time, right action that prevented a problem from happening. Why? The military calls it "situational awareness." You can call it "paying attention."

Maxim 4: If You Can't Read a Map, Find Someone Who Can; Better Yet, Find Two People Who Can

Don't count on technology to help you through your weak spots. Batteries die. Wi-Fi fails. No satellite reception. Google Maps sends you on a wild goose chase.

Are we just talking about maps here? Of course not; reading a map is a skill … and a gift. Not everyone can translate that two-dimensional representation of three-dimensional topography to navigational use. Just like not everyone can navigate Excel spreadsheets or double-entry accounting.

Everyone has weak spots. Know yours and don't be afraid to admit them. If you don't recognize your own weak spots, how can you shore them up?

Why do we need two guides, not just one? Easy. Your one guide will take a new job, get promoted, get stolen by a superior who can't read a map either! Have a backup. You will need one someday. That someday will also be a crisis day. When the GPS fails, know where the topo map, compass, and map reader are.

Maxim 5: Lead by Example, Dammit!

Each one of us has had that "Do as I say, not as I do" supervisor. How much did you hate that? Your subordinates will hate it just as much.

When I took command of the Illinois National Guard, I saw far too many overweight, out-of-shape colonels and senior NCOs sitting behind desks. They served as lousy examples to the soldiers. My goal: Get those fat butts in shape!

The Army and Air Force each have physical fitness standards, which require the ability to perform timed physical fitness tests to minimum standards, as well as weight standards. Failure to meet the standards could result in lost promotions, missed training opportunities, and poor performance evaluations. The necessity for physical fitness in the military is obvious. To perform well in combat, or in disasters, such as blizzards, forest fires, or hurricanes, requires physical fitness.

In spite of the regulations and the obvious need to maintain those standards, some people shirked the need to maintain their physical fitness, especially senior ranks assigned to headquarters desk jobs.

That first week on the job in a crisp, sunny Illinois September, I went to the cafeteria each lunch hour; bought a salad to take to my desk; then strolled to the locker room; pulled off the camo uniform; and pulled on the Army running shorts, gray Army t-shirt, running shoes; and set off running the three-mile, fenced perimeter of Camp Lincoln. Soldiers headed to lunch, soldiers returning from lunch, soldiers just smoking and joking their lunch hour away, saw the solitary figure of the "old man" (as all commanders in the military are known to their subordinates) pounding out his daily run.

Finishing the run, I didn't head immediately to the locker room for a shower. Oh, no. I strolled through the headquarters building, dripping sweat, as I greeted every soldier and civilian employee I passed. The soldiers loved it. The senior leaders, who weren't meeting the standard, hated it.

Did my little piece of showmanship work? A bit. It encouraged the soldiers who worked to maintain their fitness. It showed them the boss was committed. The fat colonels mostly stayed fat, but they knew what the boss valued.

It helps if your senior subordinates are invested in your leadership-by- example philosophy.

An example: My senior enlisted subordinate was the sergeant major, or "*the* Sergeant Major," as it's properly pronounced in the Army, when you're referring to a unit's senior enlisted soldier. In this case, John Starbody. Command sergeant major and my senior enlisted advisor for the Illinois National Guard. John is the last of an era.

From Huey door gunner and crew chief in Viet Nam to ramrodding a Chinook outfit in Afghanistan for his commander, Colonel Fred Allen, John knew soldiers, helicopters, and what made them tick and fight. He served his entire career in Army aviation until I selected him to serve as my senior enlisted advisor.

Shortly after becoming State Command Sergeant Major, John suggested that we have a division run on a drill weekend when all the full- and part-time soldiers at state headquarters would be present for duty.

"Sir," he said, "everybody knows you're a runner and always pushing physical fitness, so let's fall everybody out and do a two-mile run around Camp Lincoln next drill weekend." John and I frequently ran the loop around Camp Lincoln, making a striking pair. We were both pushing 60, with John at 6 foot 3 and 195 pounds with close-cropped white hair, while I was 5-8 and 165 with equally close-cropped, but brown, hair. As we liked to say, we had boots older than our youngest soldiers. "Hell, I got boots older than their parents," one or the other of us would growl.

"Great idea, Sergeant Major," I replied. "I'll tell the chief of staff to get it set up."

The first Saturday in October dawned crisp and cool — perfect football weather in central Illinois. Great day for a run. Soldiers from Joint Force Headquarters at Camp Lincoln and airmen from the 183rd Tactical Fighter Wing at nearby Capital Airport milled about until the NCOs started shouting at them to form up.

Four lines of gray T-shirt–clad men and women gathered on the perimeter road with me at the far right of the formation and the Sergeant Major at the far left. A young staff sergeant who'd recently graduated from the Army physical fitness instructor academy led us in warm-up calisthenics. Once properly stretched and loosened up, I took charge of the unit and set off at a brisk pace for the two-mile run with the guidon bearer, carrying the lance with its unit flag, a few paces behind me. The sergeant major, as is tradition, was at the rear of the formation to ensure no stragglers.

Several hundred yards later, the sergeant major passed the formation on the right with his long, loping stride and seized the lance from the guidon bearer. "Come on, sir, let's go!" he said. I immediately understood his challenge, wheeled to the left, and with him following, picked up my pace to sprint around the column as the soldiers and airmen cheered us on, circling the formation at a run while they maintained their measured pace along the perimeter.

John instinctively knew how to lead soldiers. We hadn't planned that sprint, but he knew that the younger soldiers would tell stories for months afterward about *the* general and *the* sergeant major running laps around the formation while running two miles. That's the kind of leader he was.

Lead by example, and make sure your senior subordinates lead by example, too.

Maxim 6: Recognize Excellence

Determine what you value in your subordinates' performance, then reward excellence. As a National Guard commander, I valued physical fitness. The ability to perform under combat conditions or under the stress of natural disasters requires a high level of physical preparedness.

The Army tests physical fitness at least once a year. A perfect score on the fitness test when I was TAG (commanding general), was three hundred. A movie about the famous battle of Thermopylae entitled "The 300" had just been released. In that battle three hundred Spartan soldiers fought to the death against a vast Persian army, holding them off, allowing the bulk of the Greek army to escape to fight again. The battle is legendary among soldiers for the bravery and determination of the defending three hundred.

Seizing on the popularity of the movie with our soldiers and the coincidence of the Spartan 300 with the Army perfect physical fitness score, we designed a black t-shirt emblazoned in red with TAG 300 in a typeface similar to the movie title. Shameless cribbing? You bet! We had an announcement made at the next weekend drill to every soldier in the Illinois Army National Guard, all ten-thousand of them, that every soldier who received a three hundred on the upcoming physical fitness test would receive a TAG 300 shirt marking them as one of the best.

For months afterward soldiers would stop me to tell me they were working out to earn one.

It wasn't a promotion. It wasn't a pay raise. It wasn't a medal. And the t-shirts didn't cost the organization much. It was recognition of excellence. It was a peer recognized symbol of achievement. It sent a message throughout the organization by using the coincidence of a popular cultural token-a movie-with an Army measurement of physical fitness.

Did a ten-dollar t-shirt inspire part-time soldiers to work out more in their free time? No, it was the prospect of receiving a symbol of exclusivity and of recognized excellence that spurred them.

Take the time to recognize excellence and make it public. As the old saying goes: Praise in public, criticize in private.

Maxim 7: Get a Command Sergeant Major

In Maxim 5, I introduced you to the command sergeant major (CSM). The CSM is the senior enlisted advisor to commanders from battalion level, usually a lieutenant colonel, commanding several hundred troops, all the way up to the four-star–general level, commanding hundreds of thousands of soldiers.

Why are CSMs needed? A conduit for information from the ranks back up to the commander is vital. People in the chain of command are generally loath to tell the whole truth, especially if it's bad news, to commanders. Why? It may be fear of adverse consequences, it may be distrust, it may be barriers to approaching commanders, whether real or imagined.

CSMs, although serving directly with the commander, are still enlisted members. They have no direct command authority, yet tremendous influence due to their relationship with the commander.

As enlisted members, CSMs can still walk among the troops, taking the pulse of an organization without the disruption that a general or colonel causes. Junior soldiers are far more likely to express their concerns to a senior enlisted soldier than to "the old man". They also have the unwritten institutional knowledge of how an organization really works, as opposed to how it works in a flow chart.

The military has a formal position, not to mention training and selection process, for CSMs. Few, if any, civilian organizations do. In a union shop, the union shop steward may well fill this position informally. In non-union shops, it may be the boss's executive assistant who fills this role; that is, if you're lucky enough to have an executive assistant in today's flattened hierarchy. It may be a senior line employee.

Whoever it is, find that person. Empower them to keep you informed, to be the upward conduit of information. But don't let the relationship become such that your CSM is viewed as your "favorite pet." That destroys the CSM's usefulness to you.

In the military, the CSM is viewed as the person who can drink beer with the troops, bourbon with the staff, and scotch with the old man. Find that person.

Maxim 8: The Seventy-Percent Solution on Time Is Better than the One-Hundred Percent Solution Late

Remember this: You will never have all the facts, all the resources you need (or think you need, or would like to have), or all the time necessary to plan. You are always going to accept some risk. Accept the risk and when you get to that seventy-percent solution and time is up, roll with it.

When is the seventy-percent solution good enough? Always … except when it's not. The Boeing 737 Max comes to mind. The Columbia space shuttle comes to mind. The Bay of Pigs invasion comes to mind.

With each of those disasters, there were warning signals. There

A gift for you

Here's the book I mentioned From Harv Koplo

amazon Gift Receipt

Scan the QR code to learn more about your gift or start a return.

Leadership in Challenging Times

SQv2nZpwcr

amazon.com

Purchase Order #: Draw
Order of June 30, 2024

Qty.   Item

1   **Leadership In Challenging Times**
       Enyart, William L --- Paperback
       B0CP2P7TGP
       B0CP2P7TGP 9798987386194

Return or replace your item
Visit Amazon.com/returns

0/Qv2nZpwcr/-1 of 1-//STL9-CART-B,/next-1dc/0/0701-20:00/0701-12:27

Smart

were cautionary voices, but those voices were disregarded in the rush to get the job done. Ignored in the rush to accomplish the mission. That's why you follow Maxim 6. You need your CSM to relay the cautionary concerns to you before you pull the trigger.

Maxim 9: Know When to Be Descriptive, Prescriptive, or Proscriptive

There is never just one management style, no one road to leadership, one path to success. Different situations, different personnel, different goals require flexible leadership methods.

For example, when planning, a descriptive method of laying out a goal may be desirable. That is, you describe the end goal and allow the staff to work out the methods of achieving the goal. This style gives your staff the most flexibility.

Prescriptive is more directive. You tell the staff what you want as an end goal and how to get there. This style may be necessary if you have a junior team that lacks the experience necessary to develop routes to an end goal.

Proscriptive is the most authoritarian. It prohibits consideration of a line of action. It sets firm boundaries for a staff.

Descriptive, prescriptive, and proscriptive generally flow down the organization. Senior leaders have a more-descriptive style, while the most-junior leaders a more-proscriptive style.

What type of style do you use? Is it the correct style? Do you have an experienced staff and workers? Is your style choking off initiative or not providing enough guidance? Consider these questions as you adapt your style of leadership to fit your team's circumstances.

Maxim 10: Most People Want and Need Leadership

To think of it as a sports analogy: Not everyone wants to be the quarterback. To be the quarterback, you have to want it. Corollary: Not everyone wants to be promoted. Some folks are terrific mechanics, but lousy shop supervisors.

Get to know your people well enough to recognize their skills and career/life goals before putting a square peg in a round hole. Don't ruin a good mechanic by making her the shop supervisor if that's not where she wants to be, even though sometimes you have to challenge people to get them to grow.

How do you tell the difference between a person who needs to be challenged versus one who is genuinely content in their position? Re-read the first sentence of the paragraph above.

I've been part of too many organizations where a new boss — or worse, set of bosses — comes in and, to "put their stamp" on the organization, immediately "re-organizes the organization" by moving people around and changing duties. Usually a bad idea. There's enough organizational trauma with a new boss without the disruption to processes and lowered morale of an immediate "re-organization."

Once you know the people and culture well enough to understand who and what needs to be reorganized, you can begin the reorganization process. But remember two things: one, most people hate change and two, change is the only constant in life.

Change is a disruptor. It will initially challenge the efficiency of any organization, no matter how beneficial it may be in the long run. Be prepared to deal with the inefficiencies of change.

Once you have a sufficient understanding of an organization to implement change, "just do it" (as the Nike ad says). Do it knowing that you will receive open, as well as hidden, opposition.

As exception to the rule that you shouldn't implement immediate change is an organization failing in its mission or coming off an extended period with a toxic boss. In cases of this nature, the new boss has probably been brought in specifically to create change right away. An immediate reorganization may be necessary to emphasize a commitment to ending a toxic culture or history of failure.

Maxim 11: When There Isn't Time To Do it Right ...

The pressure is on. You have to get it done. We needed it yesterday! Go, go, go! You know the routine. Take a deep breath. Remember the Boeing Max 737 — 346 people dead. Billions of dollars lost. A corporate reputation trashed. Repercussions throughout the airline industry. All because someone rushed the software, failed to check it properly and thought "the pilots are well-trained, they can handle it." Don't build the plane that crashes, then crashes again.

There might not be enough time to do it right, but there's always enough time to do it over.

Put the sentence above in big type. Photoshop in a picture of an airplane crash, print it out, put it above your desk, make it your laptop opening page and remember it. Point to it when someone's screaming at you, "We need it right now!"

It may not make you popular, but you won't spend your nights dreaming of people falling out of the sky.

Chapter 9:
Moving beyond survival:
growth as a middle manager

Maxim 1: Once You Walk Through The Door, Don't Try To Go Back.

Once you are promoted, you will find your relationships with former peers — now subordinates — have changed forever. You can't go back, so don't even try. You have to accept the fact that you're no longer peers, which changes the interpersonal dynamics.

You can still be friendly, but let's face facts: Once you're in a supervisory position, you're no longer friends; you're a boss and your friends are your subordinates. You've entered a new social grouping with a new set of peers.

If you try to go back, you will only frustrate yourself, because the landscape has changed and your place in it has changed. If you try, in all likelihood, your former peers will view you with distrust and suspicion. You are now viewed as no longer "part of us," but "one of them."

You're either union or management, either officer or enlisted, teacher or student. You can't be both. Don't try to be.

Maxim 2: As in Chapter Three, Maxim Three, You Learn More From Your Mistakes Than Your Successes. Go back and read it again.

It still applies, but a bit differently now that you're a manager. Now it's your turn to use subordinates' mistakes as teaching moments. Don't berate subordinates for their mistakes — remember when you made them, and use them to educate your subordinates.

By handling mistakes this way, you gain two benefits. One: Your subordinates won't make the same mistake a second time. Two: By using the mistake to mentor your subordinates, rather than humiliating them, you gain their trust and loyalty.

Maxim 3: If The Dog Goes To The Door, Let Him Out.

Huhhh? What in the world does that mean? It means pay attention to non-verbal cues. The dog can't tell you what his needs are, but he can go to the door.

People, likewise, sometimes can't tell you what their needs are, or what has to be changed. Sometimes they don't know what has to be changed. Sometimes they don't know how to tell you. Sometimes they fear telling you. But I guarantee you there will be non-verbal cues.

If someone is squirming in their seat after that third cup of coffee, you know what the problem is, so pay attention to those non-verbal cues, rather than your phone, your laptop, or your own needs. By paying attention to others' cues, you'll quickly gain a reputation for being an empathic, understanding, and caring boss. Not a bad reputation to have either in a military or a corporate world largely viewed as uncaring.

Maxim 4: Not Everyone Will Like You.

No matter how empathic you are, no matter how much you educate, rather than criticize, accept it: Your job is to ensure that everyone — superiors and subordinates alike — respects you. Respects you mentally, morally, and physically.

This doesn't mean that you have to be the smartest person in the room. Nor does it mean that you're "holier than thou." Nor does it mean you bench-press twice your weight.

What it does mean is that you're mentally acute and mentally flexible. You stand ready to be educated. You stand ready to gain new understanding.

It does mean that you act in a moral manner toward others by simply following the Golden Rule: Do unto others as you would have them do unto you.

And just as you must maintain your moral self, you must maintain your physical self. Maintaining your physical self means more than avoiding abuse of drugs, alcohol, food, and other self-indulgences. It means maintaining a level of fitness adequate for doing your job. It means having interests other than your job, the Internet, sports, or gambling.

Each day, do something to keep yourself mentally, morally, and physically fit.

Enough lecturing, let's move on to the next maxim.

Maxim 5: What To Do When Your Mentor Leaves. You Do Have A Mentor, Don't You?

Having the right mentor is, I believe, the most-important factor in a successful career. The right mentor can help you navigate the rocks and shoals bound to appear along your course.

A mentor, by definition, is someone who is more senior in an organization. The best mentor is generally two or more levels higher than you. The mentor must be someone who is interested in the success of the organization and sees that long-term success is best obtained by grooming junior members for success.

Since a mentor is, by definition, senior to you in the organization, that person is likely to leave their position before you are ready for them to leave. Maybe they get promoted beyond the point they can mentor you, maybe they get transferred, maybe they retire. Maybe (heaven forbid) they get fired. Firing is far more difficult for you to finesse than the first several options, for obvious reasons.

If your mentor leaves, no matter the reason, don't seek a new mentor immediately. Take the time to survey the landscape. If you latch on to a new mentor immediately, you will appear opportunistic and it may well not be a good match. It is, after all, a match, and like all matches, it must be a good fit. It must be someone who is interested in both you and the organization — someone who sees your success as their success and the organization's success.

Be careful about how you approach a senior person to seek their mentorship. While I was serving as the commanding general of the Illinois National Guard, a newly promoted colonel came to see me. He was no sooner seated in front of my desk than he said, "General, I want to sit in your place someday. How do I get there?"

Although I knew who he was, he certainly didn't know me well enough to begin the conversation with the statement that he wanted to replace me. As a newly minted colonel talking to a two-star general, at least three levels of command above him, a far better approach would have been: "General, thanks for seeing me today. As a newly promoted colonel, I'd appreciate your advice about what I need to do to best fill my new role in the organization."

Bluntness is sometimes necessary, but seldom appreciated. Presumption is never appreciated. Don't make the presumption that a leader two or more levels above you sees you as having the skill set to lead at their level, nor that they're interested in helping you achieve that goal.

Do presume that they want to see you succeed in your current assignment and that your success will aid them. Successful subordinates are the fuel that propels leaders up the ladder of an organization. Make it your business to succeed, thereby making your boss look good.

By the way, that's a two-way street. When your subordinates succeed, don't hesitate to reward them because that success only reflects on you. If you neglect them, they'll be far less likely to bust their butts for you.

More often than not, in my experience, the mentor picks the mentee, rather than the mentee selecting a mentor, so rather than marching into the general's office (that is, your boss's boss) and asking to be mentored, do your job in such a way that your boss's boss notices and decides you are deserving of mentorship.

Back to the firing scenario. When anyone, but particularly anyone at the senior level, gets outsourced, down-sized, right-sized, or just flat out fired, it causes stress within an organization. There are, thank heavens, few people who enjoy firing employees. The dismissal of a senior executive, or at least one senior to you, not only stresses the fired executive's subordinates; it also causes anxiety among their peers, who, after all, wonder if they're next, as well as those senior to them who have to do the dirty deed.

Once again, don't scramble to find a new mentor. First, if your mentor was fired, would-be mentors may be reluctant to be associated with an employee viewed as linked to the newly departed. You must give this linkage enough time to dissipate. Second, with the anxiety caused by a termination, potential mentors are not likely to be ready to take on a new mentee.

However, you may certainly seek out advice on your role in the altered organization. Tread gently with such inquiries until the dust settles. You probably won't know who might be next, nor may the advice-giver.

Maxim 6 — Shit Rolls Downhill

This maxim is in many ways the corollary to Harry Truman's "The buck stops here." While difficult decisions rise to the top, blame rolls to the bottom. Few leaders are willing to stop that process by saying, "I take responsibility." It's far more frequent that leaders seek to cast blame on others.

If you want to be forever respected by your troops, be that stand-up leader. Be willing to say, "I'm the supervisor, it's my responsibility." You may be surprised at your boss's reaction to that. You may well earn respect from your superiors by being willing to take the hit. After all, it spares them the trouble of blaming you.

Chapter 10:
Now I've been here awhile ...
the bad news

Maxim 1: Loyalty Is A Two-Way Street, Until It Ain't.

Dogs are loyal. People may or may not be loyal. Organizations are never loyal.

How do you get loyalty? By earning it. Bosses expect loyalty. They're not going to get it without demonstrated loyalty to their employees. Now that you've got people working under you, earn that loyalty you need to succeed in your career by taking care of your people.

My wise old mentor, Colonel Jack, often told me that a "lawyer's word is his bond." Meaning if you say something, it's the truth and you'll do what you say. That saying is true for every profession and for every relationship, whether that of employee/supervisor or friend to friend. Don't lie to your subordinates nor to your superiors. Once you've broken that bond, you can't get it back.

If you mistakenly say something that isn't the truth and later discover its falsity, acknowledge it, correct it, and — if necessary — apologize for your mistake.

Two quick stories, one about apologizing and one about truthfulness.

As a relatively young lawyer, a client for whom I'd successfully obtained Social Security disability benefits came to see me about some money he'd loaned to a person who had just died. My client had lent the deceased $700. Not a large sum of money for many, but close to a month's income for my client. Knowing the lawyer handling the estate, I called him and suggested that rather than have me go through the time and expense of filing a formal claim in probate court for the money, he simply acknowledge the debt and agree to pay it. The lawyer agreed.

The lawyer was a senior partner in a well-respected firm that specialized in probate and business matters. I dashed off a quick note, confirming that he agreed to pay the claim without the necessity of filing a formal claim, which I filed away and promptly forgot about.

Nine months later, the probate case was closed. My client called. "Where is my money?" he asked. I called the other lawyer to remind him of our agreement. "Yeah, I remember our telephone conversation, but I'm not going to pay your client, because you didn't file a claim like the statute requires," he said. "You lied to me!" I exclaimed.

I was panic-stricken. It appeared I'd committed malpractice over a $700 claim. Nothing to do but admit it to my client and pay him the $700. I grabbed the slender file to find the client's phone number when I spotted the letter to the other attorney confirming our agreement. Immediately, I called the other attorney back and said, "I've got my letter to you confirming that you agree to pay the claim without our filing. Would you like me to fax it to you?"

Silence. Then: "Yeah. I see it here in my file. OK, we'll pay the claim."

Two lessons learned.

Lesson One: Always, always, always document the file, a/k/a send the CYA letter (CYA = Cover Your Ass). Lesson Two: Don't ever trust the person who lies to you. They lied once. They'll do it again. Thirty years later I still do not trust that lawyer.

Now for the apology story. While commanding the Illinois National Guard, I once chewed out a second lieutenant in front of a major. Shortly later, I discovered that the second lieutenant had not committed whatever egregious error I'd chewed him out for.

Realizing my mistake, I decided to make it a teaching moment for my staff. I called the second lieutenant in front of the 10 a.m. chief of staff meeting, filled with twenty-five or so senior officers and NCOs from every headquarters' department.

The second lieutenant, which is the junior-most officer rank in the military, entered the room, clearly expecting the worst. I stood, put my hand on his shoulder, and announced, "Lieutenant, I owe you an apology. I chewed you out this morning for something that wasn't your fault. I know that now. I apologize."

The lieutenant, clearly shocked, mumbled, "That's OK, sir, you don't need to apologize." "No, lieutenant, I do. You're dismissed," I said.

The lieutenant hurriedly exited.

With every eye on me, I turned to the stunned gathering, "You've just watched me apologize to a second lieutenant when I wrongfully chewed him out. If I can do it, you can, too," I said. I turned and walked out of the silent group.

In nearly thirty-six years of military service, I'd never seen a senior officer do such a thing. I don't know if it had the slightest impact on the assembled group. I don't know if it had any impact on the lieutenant, other than sheer terror at being called before the assembled senior officers, but it made me feel better about mistakenly criticizing a very junior person.

I don't know if it changed in the slightest how those officers went on to treat their soldiers, but I do know that my apology spread like wildfire through the organization, showing my respect for junior soldiers and thereby inspiring their respect.

Maxim Two: "Et Tu, Bruté": Beware The Phony Friend.

For those of you who are neither Shakespeare, nor Latin, scholars, the quote is from Shakespeare's play, "Julius Caesar." Caesar speaks the words when he recognizes his friend Brutus among the assassins who stab him to death.

One of the unfortunate facts of life is the phony friend. The phony friend is invariably charming, friendly, and easy to get along with. That person is far more dangerous to you than the person who is not your "friend" — the person who clearly dislikes you. The person who makes it obvious they'd like nothing better than to derail your career.

With the latter, you know where you stand, and you know to exercise caution. You know to be careful. You know to protect yourself. It's the phony friend who pats you on the back as he slips the knife between your ribs who is far more dangerous.

How do you spot such a person? That is the difficult question. The easiest way to spot such a person is to observe how they deal with others. If you observe them charming someone as they deftly step away from a falling body, you may rest assured they won't hesitate to do the same to you.

Beware their enticements; they will flatter you, provide you with "insider" gossip to make it clear that they have the inside track with important people, and offer you the embrace of power. All of which are designed solely to disarm you.

We've all met such people. You will continue to meet such people and they will become more common as you rise in the halls of power.

How do you deal with such a person? Another difficult question. First, be friendly, but do not confide in them. Listen to their tales, but do not seek advice from them. When seeking power, go around them; do not bring them into your inner circle. As the saying goes: Keep your friends close, but your enemies even closer. Don't give them the leverage to get the knife between your ribs.

Do not, under any circumstances, allow them to become aware that you know their true nature. Their stock in trade is charm and guile. To defeat this, you must assume their coloration. Respond with friendliness, but reserve your plans, your longings, your future courses of action to yourself.

As you rise in an organization, these people will see you either as a threat, an opportunity, or both. Understand that when they attach themselves to you, it is not out of friendship nor out of respect, but out of opportunism. They will abandon you or worse at the first instant you are no longer of use to them.

Rid yourself and the organization of them at the first opportunity. Do not, however, do the deed yourself. Ensure that your tracks are covered as these people are indeed vengeful.

Do not gloat once you have rid yourself and your organization of such people, because people will still be charmed by them. Gloating is unseemly and hazardous if it angers the wrong people. Let the rookie wide receiver gloat when he scores the touchdown with the play you called. Do you ever see Bill Belichik gloat?

Maxim 3: Toxic Leaders — How To Survive Them, Avoid Them, Use Them, Kill Them (Metaphorically, That Is).

Toxic leaders. Every organization has them. You will certainly, at some point in your career, serve under one of them. Their toxicity can range from one element of their personality that impedes their subordinates and detracts from the mission to those so severe that they destroy the organization or even a nation. Think Hitler or Stalin.

I've survived in an organization with such a toxic leader that, displeased at the arrangement of folding chairs at an outdoor ceremony, the CEO picked up one of the chairs and, in the presence of hundreds of employees, threw it across the stage, spittle flying from his mouth, as he screamed that the arrangement wasn't correct. After his eventual departure, it took the organization of thousands of employees several years and two CEOs, tasked with cleanup, to recover — and I don't mean the folding chairs.

One must wonder how people with such toxicity get selected for such senior positions, but it happens every day. Your job is to survive the reign of terror. The toxic leader all too often selects and promotes similar personality types, which further compounds the organization's difficulties. Bullies beget bullies.

This toxic leader appointed a sexual predator as chief operating officer. The COO sexually harassed multiple female employees. He threatened loss of employment, and offered promotions and other blandishments to obtain sexual favors. Like many sexual predators, he could spot susceptible victims. Also like many predators, he became convinced of his invulnerability.

After several years of striking fear and loathing into female employees, he picked the wrong woman to attempt to intimidate. She filed a complaint. In the investigation that followed, he attempted to coerce her into changing her story. She reported the attempt. The FBI put a wire on her.

Even though the COO knew he was the subject of a federal investigation, he was so convinced of his invulnerability that he contacted his would-be victim yet again to set up a meeting. She agreed. Wearing the FBI wire, she met with him and he again attempted to coerce her to change her story. End result: fired, charged with witness intimidation, guilty plea, two-year prison sentence, disgraced. There is justice, but sometimes it takes too long.

What do you do when you encounter these types of toxic leaders? The first survival option is, of course, to bail out. Too often, though, that's not an option. Maybe the money's too good, maybe your spouse can't transfer, maybe no lateral move is available. Maybe you don't have a parachute (more about parachutes later).

Keep your head down. Soldiers who raise their heads draw fire. Do not become identified with the toxic leader. Know this: Sooner or later, the toxic leader's flaws will become evident not only to his subordinates, but also to the board of directors, the shareholders, the voters, or the media. Once that happens, they're toast. You don't want to be identified as part of their reign of terror. Don't be the "good Nazi." If you're seen as a loyal follower, you may well get tried at Nuremberg.

Whether you're committing war crimes or enabling Harvey Weinstein or helping a pharmaceutical company loot the pockets of citizens, it's only a question of degree of culpability, not of guilt or innocence. Most toxic bosses won't reach the scale of a mass murderer, sexual predator, or rapacious plunderer. They will simply create a bad environment to work in, so you won't be required to make a life-or-death moral judgment, but you will need to protect yourself and your subordinates.

What's next after keeping your head down and not becoming identified with the bad guys? Protect the yearlings. That is, protect your subordinates from the vagaries of toxic leaders.

If it's a serial sexual harasser, interrupt them. Do not let them be alone with your employee. Head off the inappropriate comments with work-related questions. If he's a screamer, take the abuse, not your subordinates. That's why you get paid the big bucks.

If there's an ombudsperson, inspector general, independent member of the board of directors, or senior officer, get the facts to them, ideally from more than one source. Toxic leaders don't commit just one egregious act; they commit multiple acts in front of lots of people. Find the aggrieved parties and make them your allies. Relay the facts about multiple acts to your remedy source.

Do not expect immediate relief. This is a marathon, not a sprint. The evidence must get to the tipping point before you can expect action, but once it reaches a tipping point, it will have a cascading effect. That cascading effect is why you don't want to be identified with the toxic leader.

One last point about toxic leaders: Make sure you aren't one. If you've gotten this far in the chapter, it's unlikely that you are. But let's run a quick check. Do you use employee mistakes as an opportunity to teach employees or as an opportunity to berate them? Do you tell jokes or make remarks to employees of the opposite sex that you wouldn't make in front of your grandmother? Do you do, or ask employees to do, things that you wouldn't want to read about in the local paper, defend to a "60 Minutes" reporter, or see on Facebook? If your answers meet the toxic test, it may be time to reconsider your leadership actions, as well as your moral code.

I've found that the best single question to ask yourself before taking a questionable action is the grandmother test: Would you do it, say it, or ignore it in front of your grandmother?

Had Bill Clinton remembered that, no one would ever have heard of Monica Lewinsky.

Maxim 4: The Higher You Go, The Steeper The Fall.

Organizations are like pyramids: The higher up you go, the smaller the block of people and the further you have to fall. Not to mention that your exalted position is dependent on that solid base of people subordinate to you. If that base crumbles, guess what happens. Too many people fail to realize that, or forget it, as they rise in an organization.

Your job is to ensure that your base remains rock-solid so your pyramid doesn't crumble and your actions or inactions don't get you tossed down the pyramid. Think Jeffrey Epstein or Harvey Weinstein here. Committing sexual predation is one of the quickest ways to get tossed off the pyramid. Utterly rapacious greed combined with public arrogance is another ... remember Martin Shrekli.

Maxim 5: If You're Going To Take Down A Giant, Make Sure You Kill Him.

David versus Goliath stories make great legends. They make great legends because they're so rare. More often, the little guy never takes on the giant. Or the sling slips, and Goliath is merely wounded. Wounded giants aren't friendly giants. David gets squashed. End of story.

The most famous (or infamous, depending on your point of view) mayor in Chicago's long and colorful history, Richard J. Daley, once spoke the words about taking down a giant to a young state senator named John Cullerton. Cullerton decided he should run for U.S. Congress. The incumbent representative, a fellow by the name of Dan Rostenkowski, was rumored to have ethical issues.

Cullerton ran against Rostenkowski in the Democratic primary. Rostenkowski, a household name in Chicago, with buildings named after him to this day, easily defeated the young upstart and cruised to re-election. Cullerton's political career looked doomed and probably would have been had it not been for the fact that the rumors were true. Shortly after the general election, Rostenkowski was convicted of a federal felony for misuse of federal funds.

After that conviction, and for the first time in living memory, a Republican was elected to that seat.

Rostenkowski, busily occupied with making license plates, didn't have time to seek vengeance on the young state senator, who went on to become Illinois Senate president and one of the most-powerful political figures in Illinois, and an early backer of another young Illinois state senator by the name of Barack Obama. All of which leads to the next maxim.

Maxim 6: Timing Is All, Sometimes Mistakenly Recited As "It's Better To Be Lucky Than Good."

Had Cullerton waited one more term, until Rostenkowski was convicted, he would almost certainly have become a United States representative to Congress. But it didn't end up too badly for him: He went on to serve multiple terms as an Illinois state senator and as president of the Illinois Senate, with arguably a far more-successful and effective career.

How do you know when the timing is right? You don't. That's where persistence comes in. Lincoln lost multiple elections. He only served one term in Congress, lost a Senate race, lost out on nomination for vice president, yet kept on coming back. Persistence carried the day.

The same could be said of Nixon. He lost the presidency to John Kennedy in 1960. Lost the California governor's race to Pat Brown in 1962. Yet kept coming back, to win the U.S. presidency in 1968. Of course, we don't remember Nixon for his persistence, but for his paranoia, which led him to near-impeachment and resignation in disgrace.

What people too often mistake for luck is actually preparation. You must be prepared for luck. Prepared for fortuitous opportunity. Preparation puts you in the position of recognizing opportunity and seizing it when it appears.

47

Maxim 7: Have The Moral Fiber To Deliver A Non-Selection Notice In Person.

When you're the selection authority for someone who doesn't get picked for the job or a promotion, have the guts to tell the person yourself. Don't let them find out via the ceremony naming the selectee. It may not be a fun task, but the non-selectee will respect you a helluva lot more than if you display your lack of courage by letting them be ambushed by the news.

Maxim 8: Don't Ever Let Anyone Compliment You Into Doing Something You Really Don't Want To Do.

Some promotions, some jobs, some transfers just aren't a good fit. You know it. Maybe it's too disruptive to your family. Maybe the job just isn't your forte. Maybe it just doesn't feel right. Just because it's a promotion, you don't have to take it.

Sure, flattery feels good, but if it's something you really don't want to do, don't agree to it just because you've been flattered.

Maxim 9: Dipping Your Pen In Company Ink Is Always, Always, Always A Bad Idea.

The number of generals and admirals who've been disgraced and removed for consorting with junior officers is rivaled only by the number of CEOs who've been dismissed for the same infraction.

This maxim applies not just to very senior executives, but to all in positions of leadership. If you want to date someone who works for you, there are only two possible actions: 1. Don't. 2. Leave the organization. You might ask, "How about the junior person leaving the organization?" Answer: When the romance doesn't work out, guess who's going to get sued for forcing the junior person out?

Due to the power imbalance between supervisor and subordinate, the senior person is always going to be viewed as the wrongdoer. When the romance ends, the supervisor will be the sexual harasser. This is not a career-enhancing move.

No matter how sincere the romance, it's bad for business. Other employees will view the junior employee with jaundiced eyes as gaining favoritism through the romance, while the senior will be viewed as taking advantage of their position.

How about if you're the junior employee? It's still a bad idea. See paragraph above.

If you just can't live without this romance, go find another job. The overall impact on your career just isn't worth the downside.

Chapter 11:
Develop a long-term perspective

We talked about goal-setting in Chapter 3, then about raising the bar and looking to promotions ahead in Chapter 5. Is this just more of the same? Nope. This is about developing a truly long-term perspective. The kind of perspective that you can develop only with some miles and bumps in the road behind you. The kind of perspective that can guide you to a life well-lived… if you let it.

Life is a journey. Like any journey, you are moving through a landscape. What does that landscape look like? What do you want it to look like? What matters to you? What do you want to look back on at sixty? At seventy? At eighty?

As my wife frequently asks me when I'm trying to decide whether to attend an event, "Will they be at your funeral?" That's a perspective you don't have at twenty, or thirty, or even forty. You begin to develop that perspective at fifty or later, as mortality beckons.

It's simply a view of who and what is truly important to you.

I remember well the lunch after my paternal grandmother's funeral. I was in my late thirties, and my early-twenties cousin was speaking to my uncle, his Korean War veteran dad: "Dad, I'll pay off the layaway on my VCR next week. Can't wait to get it home." His dad: "That's nice."

For those of you who don't have the slightest idea what a layaway or a VCR is, let me explain. Layaway was a popular twentieth-century method of time-payment purchase used by people who didn't have credit cards or the cash to purchase an item. The buyer made a down payment, then the merchant put the item back in storage, where it was held until the purchaser finished paying for it. Layaway enabled working-class people with no or poor credit to purchase merchandise. If the buyer failed to make the necessary payments, the goods went back on the merchant's shelf and the buyer forfeited the money they had paid.

VCR stands for video cassette recorder. You could rent movies to play on it, or record programs on television to play on it later. Once incredibly popular and a fixture in every middle-class home, they became obsolete with the advent of streaming devices.

What's the point of this little journey down technology's blind alleys? A twenty-something-year-old's perspective in chasing the latest shiny, must-have object is short-sighted. The desire of a working-class kid to prove to his parents that they were acquiring the trappings of middle-class life, clear evidence of the power of materialism in our society.

You've probably heard the maxim: "He who dies with the most toys, wins." That VCR is long since buried in a landfill. The Korean War vet, like the grandmother, long since buried, too.

Has the youngster gained perspective since? I hope so; that new iPhone will soon have a cracked case.

Know this: Someone will always have more money. Someone will always have more toys. Someone will always have more power. What will the people who bother to show up for your funeral have to say about you and the life you lived? Your leadership style will say a lot for you.

Chapter 12:
Learn to tell a story

You've made that jump from middle-management to senior executive status. If you haven't already done so, now is the time for you to develop the gift of telling a story.

For most of history, it is the storytellers who have set the culture of our societies. If you want to influence the culture of your organization, you must be a storyteller.

That story is your vision of the future. Your future, the organization's future, the nation's future. A future that invites people. A future that inspires people. A future that offers promise.

Think of the great leaders of the last couple of centuries. What were they if not great storytellers? Winston Churchill, speaking in 1942 after the battle of Alamein (the first major Allied victory of WW II), said: "This is not the end. It is not even the beginning of the end. But it is, perhaps, the end of the beginning."

Franklin Delano Roosevelt, in his first inaugural address, said: "The only thing we have to fear is fear itself."

Abraham Lincoln, in the Gettysburg address: "Four score and seven years ago, our fathers brought forth on this continent, a new nation, conceived in Liberty, and dedicated to the proposition that all men are created equal."

Douglas MacArthur, upon leaving the Philippines in defeat during World War II: "I shall return."

What are these if not stories? Each of these takes a vision — an affirmative vision — and sets it into the beginning, not just of a story, but of a legend.

Several times a year, the Library of Congress, through a privately funded grant, hosts a dinner for members of Congress and guests to dine with an author who speaks about their book. During my brief tenure in Congress, my wife and I attended one of those small gatherings at the Library of Congress, featuring the award-winning presidential biographer Doris Kearns Goodwin. She has written biographies of both Roosevelts, Lyndon Baines Johnson, and Lincoln, among others.

In a question-and-answer session after the dinner, one of the forty or so people in attendance asked: "If you could sit down with any of the presidents you've written about and ask one question, who would it be and what would you ask?"

Without hesitation, Ms. Goodwin replied: "It would be President Lincoln. I would say: 'Mr. President, tell me a story.'"

Learn to tell a story. Define your leadership style by the kind of story you tell.

Chapter 13:
The view from 35,000 feet

You're at 35,000 feet. Great! You're an executive surveying the grand scope of things. You've got the strategic view from reading all the metrics, all the reports, all the data that show you what's what. You scan the terrain below of all your campuses, or factories, or forts. They are nicely outlined with white-washed rocks. It all looks great from 35,000 feet.

Beware the white-washed rocks. Looks pretty — but what useful purpose do they serve? Are you asking for white-washed rocks? Are your people giving you what you need, or what they think you want? Are the data you want the data you need? Are you fighting the right battle?

Think Kodak. Kodak and Fuji were fighting it out for the photographic film market. A few other minor players, but they're the King Kong's of photography. Where are they today? Digital photography ended the reign of Kodachrome, not Fuji. Will Paul Simon write lyrics extolling the virtues of the pixels in an iPhone XXX?

Contrast Kodak with IBM. The IBM Selectric dominated the typewriter business a few decades ago; then IBM became a personal computer business. Today, IBM is a services company, not a hardware company. IBM sold its personal computer business to a Chinese company while completely shifting its focus. Strategic success by completely remaking itself. Strategic success by divesting itself of legacy industries while adopting a new focus.

Let's look at a military/diplomatic example. Consider Korea. 1950. North Korea invades South Korea. Completely routs the South Korean Army, as well as the Americans. MacArthur executes a brilliant, if incredibly risky, tactical move by an amphibious landing at Inchon, striking deep behind North Korean lines.

It's now North Korea's turn to collapse. MacArthur orders his forces to drive to the Yalu River, the border between North Korea and China. With the arrogance of complete control of the sea lanes surrounding the Korean peninsula, as well as the air over both Koreas, MacArthur ignores glimmering intelligence hints of the Chinese massing hundreds of thousands of troops on the Chinese-Korean border.

The Chinese are poorly equipped but have just finished seizing control of the mainland from the Nationalists, with decades of war behind them. For all their weaknesses, they have a huge numerical advantage and MacArthur's forces are driven back to the 38th parallel, where the war began. MacArthur, the five-star theatrical general of WW II fame, whose legend is only eclipsed by Patton and Eisenhower, winds up getting fired by a former National Guard artillery captain by the name of Harry Truman.

Where are we today, more than seventy years later? Still on the 38th parallel, still with tens of thousands of U.S. troops based in South Korea, still technically at war in Korea. Negotiations with North Korea drag on over their nuclear weapons program, with no progress in two decades in both Republican and Democratic administrations.

Why? The American government has focused on negotiating with Kim Jong-un and applying economic sanctions on North Korea. The North Korean government continues despite the sanctions.

Why? We're applying tactical efforts, rather than strategic ones. Korea is a peninsula attached to the Chinese mainland. Were the Chinese to apply pressure to North Korea Kim Jong-un and the North Korean nuclear program, both would be finished in weeks.

The Chinese have no interest in taking such action because North Korea is a useful distraction. It keeps the U.S. focused on a tactical problem rather than a strategic problem. North Korea is a useful yet disavowable tool for the Chinese to use.

The lesson of all this? Know who your strategic rival is, not just your tactical rival. In Kodak's case, it was a technological revolution. In IBM's case, it was a manufacturing revolution. In the U.S.'s case, it's ...?

Lesson learned: Just because you're at 35,000 feet doesn't mean you have a clear view of the future.

Second lesson learned: When somebody whispers "The Chinese are massing hundreds of thousands of troops," take a look before you shoot the messenger.

Chapter 14:
Relax, it ain't a firefight

Maxim 1: Planning.

There are those management gurus who say planning is the most important aspect of a successful career. Their advice is to have one, communicate the plan to those with a need to know, know when to revise it, know when to abandon it and most importantly have a backup plan.

I can attest to the value of this maxim because I've, more often than not, ignored it. I like to think that I grabbed opportunity as it became available and ran with the ball. I'm also miserable at communicating plans, even to my wife.

If, like me, you're not good at developing or communicating plans, what did I tell you about map-reading? If you're not good at it, find someone who is and keep them close. As I moved up in the military and in civilian life, I was lucky enough to have people who were good at developing plans and who didn't hesitate to ask me if the plan met my intent. Whereupon, I'd sagely nod my head and say yes.

The old Army wisdom says that the plans go to hell as soon as you hit the beach. In other words, once life intervenes the best laid plans go awry.

Your job is to see the big picture. Your job is to see the puzzle for what it is. So, delegate planning to planners. Your job is to sketch the vision, not to paint by number.

Knowing when to abandon a plan is set out in the old Army saying: Don't reinforce failure, reinforce success. In other words, when you've got Patton breaking through and smashing across the plains of Northern Europe, pile on the effort, don't fritter resources on another front that's not bearing fruit. Is such a strategy risky? Sure, but how did Apple, Facebook or Google get to be the titans they are? By exploiting their successes and abandoning failure.

Don't be tentative. Exploit your successes. That's why nobody, other than Civil War history buffs, knows who McClellan is, but everybody knows who Grant is.

A business plan, an economic development plan, a war plan, all are just paper. Operationalizing the plan is what matters. You will never have all the facts you need. You will never have all the resources you need. You will never have all the support you need. Your job is to know when you have just enough to pull the trigger. Then pull it.

Maxim 2: Communicate. Communicate. Communicate.

I hate meetings. I hate wasting time. I hate listening to other people's agendas, whines and cautions. BUT, sometimes it's necessary. Sit through the bullshit so that you can at least pretend you've heard it. But delegate as much of that as possible.

Your job is to set strategic goals. Your job is to develop organizational culture. Your job is to influence the vision the public, the board and employees see.

Make that vision, that message, simple. Drive it home. Always, always, always remember KISS. Keep It Simple, Stupid. Complexity confuses people.

Running large organizations and influencing events is a complex process. That's why you're in the position you're in. You understand complexity. Complexity doesn't scare you.

When you're Eisenhower invading Northern Europe, your job is to defeat Nazi Germany, not plan the load factors for C-47s carrying paratroopers or for landing craft ferrying infantrymen. Your job is to conduct the orchestra, not play first violin, nor last woodwind.

My predecessor as commander of the thirteen thousand soldiers and airmen of the Illinois National Guard took command in early 2003. The active-duty Army and Air Force were stretched thin with Iraq and Afghanistan. The Army National Guard was well into transitioning from a peace-time training force, largely used for natural disasters, with a few weeks training a year for military duties, to an operational military force trained, equipped and prepared for combat duty.

Circumstances dictated a cultural shift from peace-time training and occasional emergency responder to combat ready warriors. How do you drive that change? He adopted a centuries-old infantry command as the new motto: Fix Bayonets!

Posters with "Fix Bayonets!" appeared in headquarters and local armories throughout the state. That cry started every meeting, every drill. It ended every meeting, every drill. Now, in a world of drones, laser guided bombs and satellite imagery, bayonets are, at best, an anachronism, but that simple image of soldiers driving a bayonet home over a rifle barrel in preparation for immediate hand-to-hand combat set a tone of urgency for an entire organization.

That simple two-word message reset the thought patterns for thousands of citizen soldiers. When you're facing a dramatic mission change, when you're facing the need for a dramatic mind shift for your organization find your two-word message: Fix Bayonets!

Maxim 3: Lead By Example And Expect Your Subordinates To Do The Same.

It's not enough to lead by example, you must also demand that your subordinates do the same. If you are not requiring subordinates to also lead by example your greatest efforts die one level below you. Only if you demand that they also lead by example do you have a hope of inspiring the troops.

Soldiers look not only to your actions, but also the actions of those close to you and your immediate subordinates. If the bulk of your subordinate leaders are failing to lead by example, it shows your troops that you are not following through, which negates much of your example.

Maxim 4: If Something Wakes You At 3 AM, It's Time To Fix It.

Well, don't fix it at three am, but ASAP. There's a reason your subconscious is waking you up. It's not going to stop until you take action.

Shortly after taking command of the Illinois National Guard, I awoke at three am realizing that I had no clue as to what planning we had done in the event of a major earthquake in the New Madrid fault.

The New Madrid fault is a geological fault line that is centered under southeast Missouri and northeast Arkansas. Although well known to Midwestern disaster planners and geologists, it is little known outside that community, as it doesn't erupt with the frequency of West Coast earthquakes. However, when it does cause a major earthquake, it is of immense proportions.

The 1811–12 series of three major earthquakes caused church bells to ring in Philadelphia, caused the Mississippi River to run backwards and created lakes in the Midwest. The region was sparsely populated with little development or infrastructure then. Today, however, tens of millions of people live in the five-state region centered on the Mississippi and Ohio River junction. Major interstate highways, rail lines and barge infrastructure provide transportation links that power our nation's economy. Electric transmission lines, natural gas pipelines and coal and oil barges crisscross the region to provide the power that powers our economy.

Chemical plants, oil refineries and steel mills line the east side of the Mississippi River bank across from St. Louis from Dupo, Illinois, north forty miles to Alton, Illinois. The Mississippi River floodplain they sit on will turn to jelly in a major earthquake. The human and environmental consequences of an earthquake the size and scale of 1811–1812 will outweigh and outlast Katrina, the San Francisco earthquake of 1906 and the current crop of California wildfires put together.

Tens of thousands of casualties, disrupted transportation networks, destroyed power supply infrastructure with chemical plumes contaminating air and water are all very real probabilities. And not just in Southern Illinois, but stretching across Missouri, Arkansas, Kentucky, Tennessee and northern Mississippi. The impacts on power transmission, transportation links and industrial capacity will be felt nationwide.

Exaggeration? The US Geological Survey predicts a one in ten chance of a 7.5 to 8.0 scale earthquake in the region in the next fifty years. For a 6.0 to 7.0 earthquake in the next fifty years the probability goes up to one in four to one in two! You might want to get your emergency kit put together.

Three oh five am. Can I get my Blackhawk and Chinook helicopters into Scott Air Force Base to ferry in supplies and medics, to locate and rescue injured citizens? Can I get the relief convoys of mobilized Guardsmen bearing supplies, water and fuel over the likely damaged bridges and under the quake-shaken overpasses?

Three oh seven am. Pick up my then state of the art Blackberry (would they be working in Southern Illinois?) and email my senior disaster preparedness staff officer: "What plans do we have in place to deal with a major earthquake in the New Madrid zone? I want to be briefed on them first thing."

Second email sent a few minutes later. "Welcome to my world."

Within minutes, the response, "Yes sir."

A few hours later, I'm getting the briefing laying out the planning response and the linkages with the Illinois Emergency Management Agency (IEMA) and the Federal Emergency Management Agency (FEMA). I sleep a little better that night knowing that there is a response plan. Will the civilians be ready? Nope, they seldom are. Will the disaster response be fast enough? Will the resources be enough? Nope, you can't stockpile enough to be ready to respond to every contingency, but you can have a plan to begin the response so the resources can flow as needed.

Four weeks later I'm in Washington DC, with several staff officers, making a presentation to the three-star deputy commander of the

National Guard. "Sir the thing that wakes me up at three am is the New Madrid Fault."

"What's that?" the combat uniform clad general asked.

Maxim 5: There Will Always Be Competing Interests.

You can't always resolve them. Know when to let them play out.

You're Eisenhower. Montgomery wants troops, fuel and supplies to strike the Germans in the north. Patton wants tanks, fuel and supplies to drive across France. Same long-term goal, defeat the Nazi war machine, but competing ways to achieve the goal.

As a senior leader you will frequently be faced with competing interests. With the luxury of hind sight you'll see: I should have given the resources to Patton and let him drive on. Maybe, but then on a narrow front his supply lines might have been severed and a military disaster occurred when he ran out of fuel and ammo.

Generally, when competing interests are presented to you, they will each, or all, make sense. They will all have a probability of success. If they don't your staff is trying to force you to select a particular plan. All of which leads us to Maxim 6.

Maxim 6: Don't Let Your Staff Box You Into A Decision.

All too often I've seen three courses of action presented. One obvious, one less obvious and one obviously flawed. When I see that I know it's time to send the staff back to the drawing board. They've pre-selected a plan and built the three courses of action to ensure the one is selected.

Maybe they're doing that because they believe it's the one you favor. Maybe it's because there is a dominant person or faction in the planning process who has outsize influence. It's not far from the personnel selection committee who provides you three names. One rocket star and two mopes. They're trying to box you in to a decision. Don't let that happen.

Don't be afraid to take criticism for making a decision to not take an action. As my three-war fighter pilot law partner used to say: "There's no peace-time mission worth flying into a thunderstorm to complete."

Maxim 7: Don't Mistake Acquiescence For Agreement.

You're a senior leader. You walk into the room and the dynamic changes. You need to understand that. There are very few subordinates who do not at least shade their thoughts when you are present.

Even people who aren't the least bit reluctant to tell their supervisor an idea is full of crap start to fade when leaders two or more echelons above are the recipients of their thoughts.

How to resolve this. Stay the hell out of the room. Your job is to set a strategic goal. Let the staff work up the concepts. Let the staff work up proposals and benchmarks. Let the staff freewheel their way into designing multiple courses of action.

When the planning process is at this stage stay out of the room. If the staff needs guidance let them send a delegation. I say a delegation because it's important that it be more than one person. If it's one person returning to the meeting from the boss's office, that person speaks with the "voice of the old man (military-speak for the commander)", while two or more diffuses that appearance of authoritative voice.

During the planning stage it is more effective to ask questions than issue directives. "Have you overlooked X?" rather than "I want you to ...." Give your staff room to consider what they may have overlooked and how to factor it in.

Maxim 8: Do You Have A Command Sergeant Major?

A Command Sergeant Major in the Army is the commander's senior enlisted advisor. He or she is the ranking enlisted person in the organization and reports directly to the commander of a battalion or larger size organization. A battalion generally is 450 to 600 soldiers.

Commanders use CSM's as a two-way conduit of information to and from the troops. Enlisted soldiers will tell a Command Sergeant Major things they wouldn't tell an officer. They will also listen to a crusty old enlisted soldier before they will an officer.

Each of the military branches has a senior enlisted advisor to commanders of larger units. This tradition dates back centuries if not millennia. Militaries are often criticized for being hide bound organizations, reluctant to change traditions, but this tradition is a worthy one to emulate.

You need a trusted intermediary who workers can identify with and trust to relay information to and from you without fear of reprisal. This intermediary must have the trust of both you and the worker bees.

Your staff will fear and loath this intermediary for he has your ear. Do not allow this jealousy to interfere with your relationship with your CSM, but do keep it in mind. You must also ensure that the CSM does not overstep bounds. There is the occasional CSM who begins to believe he or she wears your rank. When that happens do not hesitate to replace him or her.

Maxim 8: Good Leaders Groom Young Leaders.

The long-term health and success of any organization, or nation, for that matter, is determined by the growth and success of young leaders. Too often, I've seen young leaders, stymied by an inability to grow, leave an organization. When that happens in the military, due to a toxic leader, we call it "eating our young".

In the Illinois Army National Guard, we did a pretty good job of recruiting young black soldiers. We did a fair job of selecting black junior officers. We did a miserable job of keeping them. Typically, young black officers left the organization as first lieutenants or captains, junior officers for you civilians, for the US Army Reserve or for civilian life. Those officers faced a virtually all white senior officer corps and a serious lack of mentorship.

As an officer moving up through the ranks of the Guard, I don't recall ever hearing explicit racist remarks but those informally chosen for mentorship had a tendency to look like and act like their seniors, i.e. white, Christian males.

A few years after I retired from the Guard, I attended a promotion ceremony for the first woman selected as a general in the Illinois National Guard. In her remarks, she mentioned several of the generals who had mentored her.

I was astonished to hear her say: "The most powerful thing I ever heard General Enyart say happened at a Chief of Staff meeting one day, when he walked in to the conference room, looked around at the thirty or so assembled officers and senior NCO's and growled: 'This room looks way too much like me. Old, white and male.' He then turned around and walked out. He delivered a message that made some people uncomfortable but needed to be said. I will never forget that moment."

Your job is to provide a ladder for success for competent young leaders irrespective of whether they look like you, worship like you, or vote like you.

Maxim 9: Never Waste A Good Crisis.

Like many a pithy saying, "never waste a good crisis" or a variation thereof, is attributed to a wide variety of authors, ranging from Winston Churchill to Saul Alinsky and others. Rahm Emanuel, then President Barack Obama's chief of staff and later two-term mayor of Chicago, in a 2008 Wall Street Journal interview said: "You never want a serious crisis to go to waste".

He was speaking of the financial crisis that nearly wrecked the world's economy and lead to the worst economic downturn since the 1930's Great Depression.

It simply means that during times of crisis people are open to ideas that they wouldn't be otherwise. When the world appears to be collapsing it is possible for bold leaders to drive through changes that people and institutions wouldn't normally consider.

Most people and institutions hate and fear change. It is only during times of upheaval that it is possible to radically change standard operating procedures.

When a crisis develops, use it. Use it to challenge assumptions, protocols and standards. During times of crisis people are not just willing, but indeed anxious to welcome a leader with bold answers. Thus, it's far easier to implement change in a time of crisis. Failing to do so wastes that opportunity.

Maxim 10: What To Do When Your Number Two, Your Heir Apparent, Isn't Capable Of Doing Your Job.

Sooner or later we all face this problem. You have a perfectly competent second in command. But that person has reached their peak. You know that for them to assume your position would invoke the Peter Principle, that is they have gotten promoted one level beyond their level of ability.

Invariably that number two believes they're capable of performing at that next step, yet you and your bosses, whether it's the board, POTUS, or your largest shareholder, realize that number two is a number two not the Alpha dog.

You will be tempted to keep the person in place. Afterall, they're good at their job. It will cause disruption in the organization to remove them and you will have to go through the pain of breaking in a new number two.

I once made the mistake of keeping a competent number two far too long simply because the pain of replacing him didn't appear worth the gain. I was wrong. I kept my predecessor's number two in place because he knew the organization and did a competent job. I knew he was not acceptable to my superiors as the CEO. I reasoned that I would replace him at a time convenient to me.

What I failed to realize is that I may have been in charge of the organization, but I wasn't in control of events.

A year prior to my private, tentative plan to leave the organization I was offered an opportunity I could not pass up. I left on six days notice to my boss, leaving my number two in charge.

He expected to become the number one. I told him he wasn't going to advance to the corner office. After dangling for six months, as the acting director, he was passed over for a new leader two grade levels below him. He then took every opportunity to undercut the new leader and sabotage the succession. Although the new leader replaced him within several months, the damage to the organization persisted for the remainder of his time in office. By the way, the new leader was nowhere on my list of potential successors.

Lessons learned: 1. You don't know what the future brings, so don't delay making tough decisions, they won't get any easier with time. 2. If you know your number two can't handle your job move them out. 3. Once you leave an organization, it's unlikely you'll have much input into the selection of your successor so make damned sure you take care of positioning the right people *before* you leave.

Maxim 11: Hey, It's Only Money.

Unless you're a battlefield commander, a heart surgeon or a juror in a death penalty case, the decisions you make probably aren't life and death matters. Remember that.

A Federal District Court Judge put that thoroughly in context for me. I was defending an Air Force colonel in a criminal case where he had allegedly defrauded the government. The prosecutors and I were struggling to reach a plea agreement. The judge held a pre-trial conference in his chambers. After listening to the prosecutors and me bicker about the case, he looked at us and said, "You know, after being a nineteen-year-old Marine Corps fire team leader in Viet Nam, not a whole lot of what I do bothers me."

The clear implication to the attorneys: this wasn't a life-or-death matter, let's get it resolved.

Keep that perspective. Balance your life and balance your decisions. You may feel like you're in a firefight, but if you're not, don't make it one.

Maxim 12: What To Do When There's No Right/Easy Decision? Corollary: The Buck Stops Here, Harry S Truman.

I've found it helpful to take a yellow legal pad, draw a line down the middle top to bottom. I list the pros on the left, the cons on the right. If there are multiple courses of action, I do the same for each one. After listing all the pros and cons I can think of, I seek input from others as to pros and cons.

I then rip the sheets off the yellow legal pad, wad them up and toss them in the trash can (or shred them, depending on their sensitivity), and go with my analytical gut.

Another alternative is to utilize the digitally operated, randomly generated, binary choice, decision determinator; that is: flip a coin.

Don't forget to add in the human costs of any decision you make. Do you close a plant throwing a thousand workers out of a job, disrupting families and communities or do you keep it open in hopes of turning it around, yet risking the company with tens of thousands of jobs? Do you allow off-shore oil drilling, providing jobs and keeping our oil-based economy moving or do you prohibit it, thereby protecting the jobs of fishermen, shrimpers, tourist-based industries and the environment? Do you keep thousands of troops in Afghanistan, accepting the risk of casualties and costs of maintaining them there or do you pull them out accepting the risk of it again becoming an ungoverned terrorist training ground?

As we in the military say: "It's a shit sandwich."

That's why I bought a replica of the plaque President Truman kept on his desk that says "The buck stops here." It's a reminder that tough decisions have to be made and I accept responsibility for making them.

That's why it's imperative that you never, never, never lose your empathy. Empathy is that ability to understand the impact on human lives that your decisions have. The ability to see the pain on human lives. If you don't occasionally wake up at night concerned about that human impact you need to get out in the field and spend some time with the troops. You need to meet their families and hear their concerns. It's people who make up your organization, not contracts, nor cracking towers, nor brigades. People. Their loyalty and their efforts will make your organization a success. Be one of them.

Maxim 13: Nothing Is Sexier Than Success. Corollary: Don't Mistake Your Title For Sexiness.

This myopia seems to affect more men than women, or at least we sure hear about it a lot more for men. Or perhaps, it's just because more men than women are in positions of power.

Irrespective of the cause be aware that there are two issues to deal with: 1. There are people who will be, or will seem to be, sexually attracted to you because you are in a position of power. And 2. You may believe this allure you magically possess is real. No, it's not. Do not allow the flattery that you receive due to your position convince you that you are now a movie or rock star. Unless, of course, you are a rock star, in which case, go ahead and live it up, just remember that sooner or later you will look like Mick Jagger.

But, if you look like Mick Jagger and are attracting the attention of young things question why. And more importantly, remember what happens to old guys and gals who take advantage of the sex appeal of their positions. You really don't want to be Bill Clinton getting impeached for Monica Lewinsky.

I know, I know, s/he really loves me. Go home. Take a cold shower. Go for a run. Imagine the two of you at your grandkids' soccer game. Does it really compute?

Chapter 15:
Pleasures of the Top Job

Remember the days when you were a grunt and had to get somewhere in the middle of Indiana? It was fly into O'Hare, rent a car, and drive three hours, unless the traffic was horrendous, and it always was, which meant drive four hours. Or fly into Cincy or Atlanta, change planes, get to Indy, rent a car, and drive an hour and a half. Yup, it was painful.

Now that you're in the top job, you just have your executive assistant whistle up the Lear or the King Air. You're driven not to the American or Delta or Southwest terminal, but to the one on the far side of the airport. The little one that no one, except the blessed — like you — is chauffeured to. Ah, yes: the one with free cappuccino and cookies. The quiet one. The one where you don't schlep your own bags, if you even are taking one (after all, it's just a quick out and back on the Lear, not a two-day slog with an overnight at the Holiday Inn Express, which has the best breakfast buffet and meets the corporate expense guidelines). Nope; if you got a bag, the porter takes it and hands it off to the crew.

The legroom in the Lear is a little tight and you'd sure like to upgrade to the Gulfstream, but your spouse doesn't want to move again.

Ahhh, yes, and the top-floor corner office suite with the floor to ceiling windows feels like home.

Don't think those perks belong to you, unless you own the company. They go with the job. They're just part of the trappings that go with the position. Eventually, you will leave the position. Remember that.

Treat the job, and the perks that come with it, with respect. We've all seen those at the very top who've become entitled. Remember how you felt about them?

Is there anyone, other than maybe his mother, who's sorry to see Martin Shrekli go to jail? The whiz kid who took over drug companies and jacked drug prices through the roof, while lording it over everyone. Don't be that guy.

Those perks are there for the benefit of the organization, to help the person leading the organization get their job done. Don't mistake it for anything else. R-E-S-P-E-C-T them. And every once in a while, have your exec book you on one of those 6 a.m. flights out of the regular airport, ideally with a change of planes, just so you don't forget what it's like for the people you lead.

Chapter 16:
Talking with Mr. Lincoln

Congratulations. You're in charge now. You're the one who gets to make the tough calls. You've done all the right things. You've had your mentors, you've recognized opportunity, you've climbed the ladder of success. You're at the top of the pyramid.

Guess what. It's lonely up there. Not many people to talk with. I said talk with, not talk at, or listen to, because you will still be listening to people, even in your exalted position. How do you handle that loneliness? That knowledge that you're making decisions that impact people's lives? I found the best way to handle it is to develop a mental relationship with an historical figure whom you greatly admire and whose advice you would love to have. Advice that would help you put things into perspective and on occasion to provide you solace.

Here's how I handled it. When I took command of the Illinois National Guard, my wife, a felony court trial judge, stayed in Belleville, Illinois, two hours away, while I took an apartment in Springfield, overlooking President Lincoln's Library and Museum. His home a few, short blocks away.

Most evenings when I was in Springfield I walked down to talk to Mr. Lincoln. Some nights it was cold, damp, gloomy. Some nights it was hot and so humid my undershirt stuck to my back. The kind of weather that would make the corn grow a foot a night, as my tenant farmer grandfather would say, while I sat spitting watermelon seeds on the back porch.

On those gloomy winter nights, with the dampness glistening on the cobblestone street, the only shadow moving on the street was mine. The sun long set in the early darkness.

On those nights I stood across the street from that pleasant, not overly imposing frame house. The only house Mr. Lincoln ever owned. Some nights, those nights when I knew I'd be alone, I wore the combat uniform of an Army officer, indistinguishable from that of an enlisted soldier. Some nights, those nights when I knew others would be in the neighborhood catching a glimpse of Mr. Lincoln's home, I stopped at my rooms, a few blocks closer to the train station he'd departed Springfield from, and changed into civilian clothes, so as not to draw attention from other visitors.

It was a private talk that I was seeking with Mr. Lincoln. Not the lingering stares of those wondering why a soldier dressed for battle stood across that quiet street from Mr. Lincoln's home.

It was a private mission, not public business, that drew me to visit with Mr. Lincoln. I much preferred to visit with him on those London-like evenings of late winter, early spring, with the chill, damp air penetrating my desert camouflage. The chattering tourists, snapping selfies, herded by guides speaking an indecipherable language or the school teachers struggling to control boisterous kids interrupted my communion with Mr. Lincoln on the warm summer nights. Good for growing corn. Not so good for a commander seeking solace.

Why did I walk to talk with Mr. Lincoln? Why did I walk from the comfortable townhouse with the fire crackling in the fireplace, overlooking Mr. Lincoln's park, and his library, and his museum, and the railroad depot he'd left Springfield from? I made that walk because he'd carried far greater burdens than I. He'd lost far more soldiers than I. Like me, a man from humble background. Like me, a working-class man who'd become a lawyer. Like me, a man who'd served as an enlisted soldier. Like me, a man who became an officer in the Illinois National Guard. Like me, a man who'd ordered soldiers into combat. But a man who'd faced far greater challenges, far greater losses than me. A man who surely could help me.

When you're a kid growing up in Illinois, especially central Illinois, you grow up with Mr. Lincoln. The license plates on your parent's car, your grandparent's farm truck and your wild uncle's motorcycle all say: "Land of Lincoln". The pennies you collect have Mr. Lincoln on them. In the sixth grade you board the big yellow school buses and trundle over to Springfield where you visit that same Mr. Lincoln's home, his tomb and the old Capitol where he sat as a state legislator. Twenty-five years later, after active-duty military service, you don the uniform of the Illinois Army National Guard and wear the patch bearing Mr. Lincoln's likeness on your right shoulder. The patch the enlisted soldiers jokingly refer to as "Abie baby".

So, it's only natural that after another twenty years pass that you turn to Mr. Lincoln for guidance. For comfort. For wisdom. I talked. He listened.

The talks with Mr. Lincoln didn't come quickly or easily. But once they started, they were very necessary. They eased my soul. They helped me get to sleep on those nights alone in Springfield. Those nights with a Blackberry by my bedside praying that it wouldn't ring during the night.

Being a general with soldiers in combat is like being a father with teenagers, when the phone rings in the middle of the night you know it isn't good news.

It was the fall of 2007 when I became the Adjutant General for the Illinois National Guard, put on the second star of a Major General and took command of the 10,000 soldiers and 3,000 airmen of the Illinois Army and Air National Guard. The military, with the Guard and the reserves had been at war for six years. The nation less so. No draft. No war taxes. No full-scale mobilization.

The Army was stretched thin. Large-scale deployments of the National Guard were taking place to spell the soldiers of the active-duty Army.

The 3,500 soldiers of the Illinois Army National Guard's 33rd Infantry Brigade Combat Team were slated to mobilize the next year for deployment to Iraq. Units of the Illinois Army and Air National Guard, like National Guard units nation-wide, had been deploying, fighting and dying, since September 11, 2001.

But this was to be our largest combat deployment since World War II.

Iraq was quieting down. The four hundred infantrymen of our Second Battalion, 130th Infantry Regiment, the same unit I'd served in as a young first lieutenant, the unit we called "two uh the one three oh", had just returned from Iraq without taking a single casualty. Maybe we've won the Global War on Terror, as the George W. Bush administration labeled it.

Six weeks into command. Six weeks after leaving my comfortable law practice. Six weeks after pinning on the second star and becoming a full-time Guardsman and no longer a weekend soldier, a half dozen of my senior colonels filed into my second-floor corner office on Camp Lincoln to ask me to agree to a re-missioning of the 33rd Infantry Brigade.

The Army didn't need us in Iraq anymore. It was quiet. The Army needed us in Afghanistan.

Afghanistan.

 Every good soldier is a student of history.

Afghanistan.

The country that hadn't been conquered since Alexander the Great. The country that killed every British soldier, but one, in a regiment retreating from Kabul through the Khyber Pass.

Afghanistan.

The country that defeated not one but two of the world's greatest empires in the last century and a half. The British and the Soviet Union.

Afghanistan.

The place where British soldiers grimly told newcomers to save their last bullet for themselves. "You don't want to be taken alive," they said.

Afghanistan.

The place where empires go to die.

I glanced around the conference table at the eager faces of the colonels. Excited to take on this new mission. Excited to face the challenge. Ready to prove to the Taliban, ready to prove to Afghanistan, ready to prove to the world, most importantly ready to prove to the Army what the Illinois National Guard and its soldiers could do.

They were thinking about the resources we'd need. The training dollars. The equipment. The chance to prove we citizen soldiers, we weekend warriors, could send a full brigade of infantrymen into battle. Some wore combat patches signifying they'd spent a tour or more in the war zone. Some didn't. They were all thinking about how to get the unit ready. None were thinking about what the job meant.

When the lead colonel finished speaking, I quietly said, "You know this means we'll take casualties." Uncomfortable silence. Colonels shifting their glances to one another. "What the hell does the old man have to ask a question like that for?", clearly hit their minds. That's why soldiering is a young man's game. Young men are convinced they're bullet proof. Old men know better. Broken bodies and bitter mothers are the true fruit of war not valor and glory. Mr. Lincoln knew that. My colonels were to learn that. Mr. Lincoln and I were to talk about that.

Find your Mr. Lincoln to talk with.

Chapter 17:
Losing James

For those of you seeking leadership level in the military or at the highest levels of the federal government, know that at some point you will order men and women into life endangering situations. Be prepared not just to do so, but also for the aftermath, the impact not only on them and their families, but also on you. Know that people will lose their lives in the course of following orders you will give.

If you are a civilian read this to gain a perspective you may not otherwise receive.

The card came a week or so before Christmas. The envelope was addressed only to Major General William Enyart, not the usual address with both my name and my wife, Annette's, but I recognized the return address and last name.

A typical holiday greeting card in this day of Internet ordering. Front of the card, a photo of two boys, six years old or so. Short-haired, tow-headed, dressed alike, as twins so frequently are. Their Scots-Irish-English ancestry clear in their faces, so common across the swath of Middle America that Southern Illinois lies in. One just a little shorter than the other, with an open-faced smile. The other more reserved, closed. Clearly the apples of their family's eyes.

A simple "Merry Christmas" below the photo. No names. No other salutation. Flip the card over, three other photos of the same two boys, same outfits, different poses. No family groupings. No mom, nor dad, nor grandparents, not even a puppy. Just the two boys.

No signature. No handwritten wishes for a Merry Christmas, nor Happy Holidays. Just the double-sided card with photos of two All-American boys. I hadn't seen those boys in person since they were toddlers, although I had watched them grow through their mom's Facebook postings.

The card sits now in the three-ring binder that holds the draft of this book. It didn't go into the recycling bin with the rest of the holiday cards. Some cards you just don't throw away.

I know from Facebook that their mom has remarried. Her new husband looks like a good man. A kind man. He looks like he'll throw balls with them. Teach them to slide into first base and take them to church every week in their tiny southern Illinois town.

I've never met him. I probably never will. I've met their mom on a couple of occasions. It was their dad whom I knew. He too was a good man.

He served four combat tours. Twice in Iraq. Twice in Afghanistan. I signed the orders sending him the fourth time. That Army Staff Sergeant was a rock. His commander in Afghanistan, Colonel Fred Allen — a rock of a man himself, a farmer, a helicopter pilot, my chief of staff — told me at the funeral that NCO was a rock. A soldier who could always be relied upon. A soldier who never quit. A soldier you wanted on your right flank.

He was quiet. He didn't say much. I never saw him get angry and God knows there were lots of times in the five months we worked side by side, after he came home from war the last time, that people got angry and rightfully so. Yet he never did. He was a rock. I never heard him swear. He was a rock. I never saw him take a drink. He was a rock.

He was one of the thousands of men and women whom I sent off to war. He came home from war. He came home not with the bloody wounds that earn a Purple Heart, the combat medal that signifies a combat wound, but with hidden wounds.

I don't know what he saw in those four combat deployments. We never talked about it. We had moved on. We were fighting another campaign. And he didn't talk much anyway.

That soldier had nineteen years in the Army and the Army National Guard. One more year for that "golden" twenty years. The twenty years that mean a pension and healthcare for life. He didn't make it. He died at the age of 41. He died in his pickup truck, empty whiskey bottle by his side. He couldn't control his demons, they told me.

His twin boys will know his name but little else, other than visions from fading photographs and stories their mother and grandparents will tell them.

I didn't cry at my mother's funeral. I didn't cry at my father's funeral. I didn't cry at my only brother's funeral. I cried at that funeral. I cried as I wrote this. It's not a pretty sight to see an old general cry. It's not a pretty sight to see old veterans cry when they talk about the friends they lost. But I understand why we do. Even God cried as we walked away from that grave — as the sun shone on that hillside surrounded by cornfields, a cool summer rain began to fall.

I couldn't talk to the soldiers at that funeral. I could only grip their arms and squeeze. I couldn't talk to the young mother of his sons as she stood in front of his casket. I could only whisper.

As a mourner, I was supposed to be consoling her, but it was she who consoled me. I whispered, "I let him down." She said, "No, we all tried. We couldn't save him from his demons." That word again. Demons.

Four combat deployments will do that. They will plant demons. I don't know how to fight demons. I know many who have tried. Tried with drink; with drugs; with 2 a.m., full of drugs and drink, on hundred mile an hour motorcycle rides. I've buried too many of those. We've buried too many of those young, and old, soldiers.

These are the weary words of an old general who has signed the orders sending young men and women to a place where, like Hell, demons lurk. Some do not return. Some return with demons. We cannot blame the VA for not saving them. We cannot blame the government for not saving them. We can only blame ourselves for sending them and then failing them.

You, too, will make decisions that will affect others' lives. You may not send people to war, but you will make decisions that try your subordinate's souls. You, too, will grieve about those adverse effects that your decisions will have on people's lives. Make those decisions as honestly as you can. Make those decisions with the best information you have. Make those decisions in such a manner that years from now, you can tell yourself at 3 a.m., "I did the best I could."

I do not regret sending James to war. I do regret not fighting more for him once he came home. I regret not seeing the demons that plagued him. I regret not standing with him in his fight with those demons. As President Lincoln said in his second inaugural address, it is our duty "to care for him who shall have borne the battle." I failed in that duty.

Know that with power comes responsibility. Exercise that power so when you are judged, here or in the hereafter, you will not be found wanting. That will be an honorable legacy as a leader.

Chapter 18:
Old soldiers never die,
they just fade away ...

If you're a young leader you can skip this chapter. Or delay reading it until later. Or go ahead and read it to plant the seed for later years. But if you're approaching career's end, here are a few considerations for you.

In the military, most promotions and prestigious assignments occur by board action. A person is nominated for promotion or applies for a select training program or prestigious assignment. A board of officers reviews the applicants or nominees and selects the best qualified. The lucky ones get a "select" letter, the remainder get a "non-select" letter. Sometimes the select/non-select letter is for retention — that is, the person is retained in their position, but if not, they must retire.

Due to the necessity to promote young officers and non-commissioned officers (NCOs or non-coms), the military has a relatively strict "up or out" policy. Thus, the need for "retention boards."

When my great friend and mentor approached the five-year point as a major general, he told me more than once that "sooner or later, even the greatest career ends in a non-select letter." He could have stayed a few more years and eventually received that letter, but instead, he faced the fact that he would never receive the third star of a lieutenant general and elected to retire at his own choosing. Doing so gave him a much-greater impact on the selection of his successor than had he been told to retire.

Maxim 1: Exit The Stage Gracefully; Don't Burn A Bridge You Might Have To Re-Cross.

We've all seen those folks who leave kicking and screaming. Left a bad taste, didn't it? How likely is it that person will be asked to come back as a consultant or sit on an advisory panel — or even get invited to the holiday party?

Even when you don't want to go, grace and dignity are the only path to walk.

Maxim 2: Be A Scout: Be Prepared. Write A Book.

The motto of both the Boy and Girl Scouts is: Be Prepared. Be prepared to walk off the stage. Whether it's a large stage or a small one, be prepared to walk off and take a seat in the audience. It will be a relief. Lead the audience in applause for those still on the stage (or lead the boos if that's what's necessary).

When all else fails, write a book. It will keep you busy, assuage your spouse's concerns about your lack of things to do, and give you an excuse not to go to the grocery store. If you've kept notes over the years about what did and didn't work when you were in command, no matter what level you reached, you have the makings of that book. You have the means to educate and inspire others. Sit down and get to it.

Maxim 3: Money, Power, Glory: When Is Enough Enough?

This is more a question each of us must ponder than a maxim, but knowing limits is invaluable for a leader. The trade-offs we make in life can't be undone. Contemplate for a moment Midas, the legendary Greek king who desired that all he touch turn to gold. The wish granted, everything he touched turned to gold — even the food he attempted to eat and the wine he tried to drink. Yup: starved to death.

Consider Alexander the Great. Conqueror of the largest empire in the world up to that time. Ruler of lands, people and armies from Greece to the Indus Valley. It collapsed after his death.

Consider Napoleon. He sold the Louisiana Territory, a swath of land that ranged from the Gulf of Mexico to Canada and from the Mississippi River to the Rocky Mountains, for $15 million to help finance his European wars. His life ended on a rocky island prison after he lost the gamble of a lifetime. The same gamble Hitler lost. The invasion of Russia.

Consider Churchill. He held on to see Hitler defeated, crushed between Stalin and Roosevelt. He won the war, yet then immediately lost office and witnessed England's loss of empire and hegemony to the land of his mother's birth: the United States.

Consider General Motors. In the 1950s, it was so large, wealthy, and powerful that its success was viewed as synonymous with the nation's. Fifty years later, it was bankrupt and preserved only through government intervention.

What will be said of you?

Conclusion:
Gramma done told me ...

We've talked a bit about the do's and don'ts of leadership, about how to progress — and not progress — in your career, and some pretty obvious ideas for how to rise in an organization. The most-succinct advice I can give you is to take 10 seconds before you make a decision and ask yourself, "What would my grandmother say if she knew I did this?"

The corollary to that advice is, "If you don't want her to read it on the front page of the local paper, don't do it." Your grandmother, by the way, probably still reads the local paper.

I can state this with some certainty because even though I don't know your grandmothers, I remember mine and the impact they had on my life and moral development well.

My grandmothers were two very different women. My maternal grandmother was a teetotaling, non-smoking Southern Baptist who went to church twice a week and whose strongest curse word was "fart." My paternal grandmother, on the other hand, smoked Winstons, loved a Falstaff or two (or three), and considered the smoke-filled bingo hall at the Moose lodge as her weekly church service. Yet they both had a strong moral code: Do what is right, don't lie, and stop hitting your little brother.

As I look back on my life and rise from kid in patched blue jeans earning a couple of bucks a week mowing neighbors' lawns and delivering the local daily newspaper to leader of an organization with 13,000 employees, a $650 million a year budget, and multi-billion-dollar property inventory, I see the mistakes I made. I would have avoided every one of those mistakes if I had followed this simple advice. If you wouldn't do it in front of your grandmother, don't do it.

Assess your leadership style through that lens, and you — and your organization — will be much the better.

About Major General (ret) William L. Enyart

Major General (ret) William L. Enyart served as Southern Illinois' United States Congressman in the 113th Congress where he served on the House Armed Services Committee and the House Agriculture Committee. He retired from Congress in January 2015. He frequently speaks on leadership, veterans' issues and defense policy. His podcast is available at billenyart.com and all major podcast providers. He is a regular commentator on military and foreign affairs on NewsNation cable network news.

General Enyart's nearly 36-year military career included active duty service in the US Air Force and nearly 30 years in the Army National Guard. He culminated his service as Adjutant General of the Illinois National Guard, commanding both the Air and Army National Guard from 2007-2012. In that role he oversaw the largest Illinois National Guard deployment of troops overseas since WWII when the 33rd Infantry Brigade Combat Team deployed to Afghanistan. He also led in-state disaster response including mobilizing hundreds of troops to assist during ice storms, blizzards and flooding in Southern Illinois. Prior to his selection as Adjutant General and promotion to Major General, where he had oversight of 10,000 Army soldiers, 3,000 airmen and more than 300 state employees, he served as a Brigadier General and Deputy Commanding General of the 10,000 soldiers of the Illinois Army National Guard.

During his military career, General Enyart participated in United Nations Peacekeeping Operations training at the UN in New York City and was a keynote speaker at the UN Peacekeeping Operations seminar in Chicago. He is a graduate of the Harvard University, Kennedy School of Government Executive Education program on US-Russia Relations. He had oversight of and training responsibility for multiple overseas deployments including; KFOR (Kosovo), MFOR (Sinai) and others. General Enyart had planning, training and oversight responsibility for 4,000 National Guard forces from 11 states at the largest NATO conference ever held, and the largest national security event ever held outside Washington DC, at the 2012 NATO conference held in Chicago. At that conference General Enyart was presented with the Commander's Cross of the Republic of Poland by President Bronisław Komorowski, for his work in building international relationships. As a Colonel he commanded the Illinois National Guard delegation to Kiev, Ukraine participating in exercises with 22 nations. During his military and civilian careers General Enyart has served in or visited thirty nations in Asia, Africa, Europe and South America, including Afghanistan, Kosovo and the Sinai.

He holds a bachelor's degree from Southern Illinois University-Edwardsville, a juris doctor from Southern Illinois University School of Law, a master's degree from the US Army War College and an honorary doctorate from Lindenwood University-Belleville.

In his civilian career General Enyart has held positions at the CEO, board and general counsel level. He taught business law at Southwestern Illinois College and business management at Lindenwood University-Belleville.

He is married to Judge (ret) Annette Eckert who is the director of the St. Clair County Teen Court. They have two sons, Dr. James Enyart, a biology professor at Southern Illinois University-Edwardsville and Alex Enyart, an attorney.

Acknowledgments

You wouldn't be holding this book if my wife, Annette, hadn't alternately cajoled, browbeat, encouraged and challenged me to finish it. Likewise for my dear friend, fellow memoirs class writer, and cheerleader, Rose Jonas. Her wit, gift of words and wise counsel kept me on the path.

Oft-quoted and always missed, my three-war fighter pilot law partner, Colonel Jack Gianninni was truly of that "greatest generation". He was wiser than he knew and the kind of mentor that every young officer and young lawyer needs. Fly high and may your skies always be CAVU, Colonel.

Major General Randy Thomas, mild-mannered high school librarian, Vietnam veteran, Special Forces, Combat Infantryman, Bronze Star, Purple Heart, friend. From lieutenants together to generals together we plotted, worked and fought to make the Illinois National Guard a better organization, an organization worthy of its soldiers and airmen. I owe you, Thirty Six. Thirty-seven out. (Randy was the thirty-sixth Illinois National Guard Adjutant General. I was the thirty-seventh. Our nicknames for each other became "36" and "37".) I'm proud to be able to say: We soldiered together.

Command Sergeants Major John Starbody and Howard Robinson you made me a better general and the Illinois National Guard the superb organization it is today. Soldier on.

For the nineteen soldiers who gave up their lives during my command that others might live: *Greater love has no one than this, that one lay down his life for his friends.*

Made in the USA
Monee, IL
30 June 2024

60972936R00049